BUYER BEWARE

Insider Secrets You Need to Know before Buying Your Home– From Choosing an Agent to Closing the Deal

Carla Cross

D1396711

Real Estate
Education Company®
a division of Dearborn Financial Publishing, Inc.

This publication is designed to provide accurate and authoritative information in regard to the subject matter covered. It is sold with the understanding that the publisher is not engaged in rendering legal, accounting, or other professional service. If legal advice or other expert assistance is required, the services of a competent professional person should be sought.

Acquisitions Editor: Danielle Egan-Miller
Managing Editor: Jack Kiburz
Interior Design: Lucy Jenkins
Cover Design: DePinto Studios

©1998 by Dearborn Financial Publishing, Inc.®

Published by Real Estate Education Company®,
a division of Dearborn Financial Publishing, Inc.®

Printed in the United States of America

98 99 00   10 9 8 7 6 5 4 3 2

Library of Congress Cataloging-in-Publication Data

Cross, Carla.
    Buyer beware: insider secrets you need to know before buying your
home—from choosing an agent to closing the deal / Carla Cross.
        p.   cm.
    Includes index.
    ISBN 0-7931-2851-X
    1. House buying—United States.   2. Residential real estate—
United States—Purchasing.   3. Real estate business—United States.
I. Title.
HD255 IN PROCESS   98-9528
643'.12—dc21   CIP

Real Estate Education Company books are available at special quantity discounts to use as premiums and sales promotions, or for use in corporate training programs. For more information, please call the Special Sales Manager at 800-621-9621, ext. 4384, or write to Dearborn Financial Publishing, Inc., 155 North Wacker Drive, Chicago, IL 60606-1719.

Dedication

To my sister, Laura Bruyneel. Through everything she does, professionally and personally, Laura is a positive influence in people's lives. If everyone had a sister like mine, the world would be a better place.

Contents

u

Acknowledgments

It tickles me when someone I know says, "I read your book. I could have written it." I take that comment as a compliment—I think it means I was able to put into words that person's feelings and personal perspective. I've gotten that kind of feedback several times, and it got me thinking about what books really are—I believe they are a collection of many people's experiences, entrusted to one writer to organize and portray faithfully in hindsight. That's a different view than I used to have. I used to think that all that knowledge must come straight out of an author's head, with little or no assistance or input! From writing, I've learned a book is a reflection of the author's experience with those in his or her life; it's an opportunity to acknowledge the lasting impact others have made, both personally and professionally.

This book reflects a collective effort from real estate professionals who want to educate buyers and raise the standards of our industry. I'm always pleased, yet somewhat amazed, that the successful professionals I mention here have been so willing to give their time and expertise to contribute to this and others of my books. Several took the time to meet with me, and to give the advice offered to you throughout this book. First, my thanks to the panel of agent advisers whom you'll see mentioned throughout. I met with them to find out how they felt buyers were coping with agency law changes, and with buying in general through this turbulent era of change. This panel was assembled by April and Steve Kieburtz, owners of Windermere Real Estate/Northwest, Inc., from among their agents in the Puget Sound, Washington, area.

The agents on the panel were chosen by the Kieburtzes because they are experienced professionals, knowledgeable about buyer agency. They are models for the kind of agent I suggest you choose when you're buying a home. Here are my panel members:

- Al Johnson, associate broker, assistant manager, Mt. Baker office

- Pam Johnson, assistant manager, associate broker, Premier Properties director, Madison Park office
- Michele Layton, sales associate, Madison Park office
- Christina Lorenz, associate broker, Madison Park office
- Kate Reiss, GRI, AB, CRS, assistant manager, Madison Park office
- Karyn Sandbeck, GRI, ABR, associate broker, Ballard office
- Susan Sellin, associate broker, Madison Park office

To me, Steve and April Kieburtz are model real estate office owners. It's been my pleasure to work with them and their management team. With her sharp mind and systematic approach, April has been instrumental in creating agency laws and practices, both in Washington state and throughout the nation. I appreciate April and Steve's support, and especially their help in writing this book. My thanks, too, to the manager of the Kieburtz's Madison Park office, David Hale, who coordinated meeting of agent advisers, and added his manager's perspective.

Another agent greatly contributed to the book. Thanks to Mark Warren, Windermere Real Estate, West Seattle, on whom I relied to contribute information about inspectors, Web sites, and the importance of being preapproved for a loan before you look for homes. I was Mark's manager for four years, and found him to be an exceptional coach for new agents (he's even on my audio program on real estate coaching). Mark is the kind of agent who keeps relationships for life with buyers and sellers.

Two real estate buyer agency educators, experts on this subject gave me valuable information from their perspectives to pass on to you. My thanks to Jeff Nelson, CRB, CRS, ABR, and Marcie Roggow, CRS, CCIM, ABR, GRI, owners of Creative Learning Concepts, Sioux Falls, South Dakota. Their educational company produced an excellent video on agency relationships for buyers and real estate professionals. It's mentioned in the "Other Helpful Sources" section of this book.

Finally, my thanks to Danielle Egan-Miller, my editor on this project, for kindly, yet firmly, prodding me to complete this project, and offering the kind of expert advice that makes a book come alive.

Together, we've given you information we hope will provide a buying experience that's positively memorable.

Preface

Never has the homebuying process been so complex. If you bought a home a few years ago and are buying another today, you'll see dramatic differences in every part of the process. If you're buying your first home, you'll be amazed at the myriad operations, paperwork, and people involved. We're in the information age, the technology explosion. With the help of computers, the homebuying process should be simplified, not made more complicated. To some extent, that's true. What's simpler and faster is the communication of the information that goes with the transaction.

Everything else is more complicated. I've experienced huge changes from the "inside," because I've been a real estate salesperson, manager, speaker, and writer for more than two decades. Twenty-five years ago when I started selling real estate, the agreement buyers signed stating the terms to purchase a home was only one page in length. Today, the agreement can extend to ten pages or more (and that's small-type legalese). Not only that, the wording of these agreements changes rapidly to keep up with new laws and regulations. It's a major challenge for real estate professionals to keep up with what the forms say, much less what the new law means!

More information about purchasing homes is available to you today than ever before. That's the beauty—and the curse. There's so much information available today, it's easy to get confused. For most of us, there aren't enough hours in the day to prioritize that information. A futurist might say we don't need more information today; we're getting too much information. Our greatest need is to *prioritize* it. (You know what I mean if you remember the amount of mail—or e-mail—you got yesterday.)

I wrote this book to help you prioritize, differentiate, and judge the information you'll be getting as you buy a home. Much of that information will come from real estate agents. As you start your home search, you'll ask agents to provide you with information about properties and the homebuying process. If you're like the vast majority of buyers, you'll have an agent assisting you in your purchase. According to recent National Association of REALTORS® (NAR) figures, 81 percent of homebuyers used a real estate salesperson to purchase a home. Unfortunately, buyers still think their main choice in the homebuying process will be to find a property they like. I think they have a different choice, a choice that directly affects their buying decision: To choose the right agent. Why? Because so much information prioritizing comes from the real estate agent. Buyers rely on agents' judgments to make decisions.

From my observations inside the industry, homebuyers aren't being choosy enough in picking an agent and are often disappointed in the level of service they receive. When asked whether buyers would use the same agent to purchase in the future, almost one-third of the homebuyers in the NAR survey said "no."

I want buyers to be pickier when they choose an agent—as picky as they are about properties! I'll give you solid criteria to use in choosing an agent, and strategies to keep your partnership on track. I'll even tell you when to sever the relationship with the agent, so you can get out of a bad situation before it becomes unbearable. I know my real estate friends may be appalled at the next statement. I believe you're better off *without* an agent than with an unskilled sleazy salesperson! However, with a competent agent, you'll get the best of all worlds—the information you need, good advice, and the right property decision for you. In this book, I offer the tools you'll need to sort the information and choose your agent wisely. In the end, I want you to be so satisfied with your choice of agent that you'll choose to work with that agent again—and provide referrals to that agent. Armed with accurate, prioritized information, much of which will be provided by a real estate agent, you can make a good buying decision.

You'll learn many "insider secrets," observations from my side of the fence that you need to recognize to protect your best interests. Why would I let you in on industry secrets? Because I want you to be able to recognize a competent, trustworthy agent when you meet one. I want you to be able to avoid the sleazy sales spiels and old-fashioned tactics some agents try on buyers to get them to work with them, or to buy a particular property. There's a saying in marketing: "The customer doesn't know what he's getting—until he doesn't." I don't want you to find out later that you didn't get what you should have during the purchasing process. This book will help you pinpoint what you ought to get—and how to get into control if you're not getting it.

Won't this book be detrimental or negative to the real estate industry? After all, I'm letting you in on some of the tricks of the trade, tactics some real estate agents and companies are still using to rake in the profits. Yes, the book will be detrimental to sleazebag companies and agents. In fact, I hope that when buyers challenge the dirty tricks revealed here, it will discourage agents from using these unethical ploys. As detrimental as the advice in the book may be to poor agents, it will be supportive to the competent, professional practitioner. I've worked in two fine, high-quality real estate companies. Now I help real estate management teams and agents across the nation put to work the philosophies and behaviors that delight clients and bring return business and referrals. From my experiences in real estate, I know there are many consumer-focused companies and agents in the industry. In fact, when real estate sales is practiced well today, it's never been better for consumers. Unfortunately, because of the changes we're all experiencing, from business to personal life, it's more difficult than ever for the consumer to pick out the "good guys" from the bad.

If real estate companies and agents are making money using the tricks in the insider secrets, what's wrong with that? It's business, after all, and the bottom line in business is to make a profit. True, but for businesses to endure through change, they must provide services that consumers find valuable. Right now, consumers have told the real estate industry that they're not thrilled paying the commissions they've been paying for the treatment they've received. In a recent Gallup poll survey, consumers were asked to rate their overall customer satisfaction in 25 professions. The real estate industry scored 19th out of the 25 professions (number one was the highest). Not a lot of bragging rights there. So, in my opinion, what's good for you, the consumer, is good for the industry. If a real estate agent provides you with a high level of customer service, you will probably be so pleased you'll refer other buyers to your agent and his or her company. Strong customer satisfaction that begets referrals, according to the business gurus, is the only way businesses will survive in the next century.

You'll see comments and quotes from real estate agents, managers, and owners throughout the chapters of this book. You might wonder why a group of real estate professionals would take the time to contribute to what some real estate practitioners would term an "exposé." The answer is that these agents, models for the kind of agent I want you to find, wanted to communicate to buyers how a competent agent practices real estate. They provided valuable advice to you about interviewing, choosing, and evaluating an agent—advice I've included in the text and in checklists for you to use in interviewing agents. I asked each agent, "How can good agents help buyers realize when they're being 'had'?" The answer, I think, lies in buyers educating themselves prior to getting into the fray of the purchasing process. I hope that real estate agents, as well as buyers, will use this book to start that education.

Besides these "insider secrets," I've provided checklists, flowcharts, graphs, and real-life stories to make your buying process easier. I've also provided two ways for you to get insights into how you prefer making buying decisions—and how your buying partner's style may differ. You'll find coordinating the process and your needs with a buying partner to be one of the most challenging parts of the buying process. You can imagine the conflict caused when you're ready to buy, but your buying partner is still gathering information! Buying a home is one of the most stressful situations we humans find ourselves in—right up there with marriage and divorce (I've even seen buying a home *cause* a divorce!). Putting to work the principles in this book can save you a great deal of stress.

In this book, you'll see statistics taken from studies by the National Association of REALTORS®. The largest professional organization for real estate licensees, NAR has as its members about half the total licensees in the United States (750,000 out of 1.5 million). I've taken statistics from several of their latest research publications to give you an idea of buyer habits and real estate trends.

As you read this book, you'll notice when referring to an agent I've randomly chosen "he" or "she." I've attempted to mix up the sexes with positive and negative stories and information. The choices aren't meant to indicate that one sex or the other is a better choice as an agent for you! I've chosen to label an agent as a he or a she simply to make the story more meaningful.

There are many aspects of purchasing a home that I've not attempted to address in this book, such as financing methods, home inspection details, or moving strategies. You'll find those in other top-notch books, many by this same publisher. What I have done is to provide information not available in any single source; how to choose, partner, and manage the buying process with a competent agent. Managing the process in the way I've described ensures that you make the best buying decision that satisfies your financial and emotional needs.

My blueprint for homebuying even will help you have fun throughout the process.

I'd love to hear from you about your particular buying experience, or with comments on this book. You can contact me by e-mail at carlacrs@wolfenet.com, or by writing to me at 1070 Idylwood Dr. SW, Issaquah, WA 98027. My best to you for an exciting and pleasant home-hunting adventure!

1

Times Have Changed Since Your Last Real Estate Transaction!

When was the last time you bought a home? If you're like most Americans, it's been at least a few years. In fact, the time between buying homes is increasing. A few years ago, Americans moved every five years. Now, Americans stay in their homes over twice as long. No matter if you bought even three years ago, chances are your next buying experience will be different in many ways.

Maybe you're reading this book because you're thinking about buying your first home. You're not alone. First-time homebuyers account for almost half of all home purchasers, according to a recent survey by the National Association of REALTORS®. In a way, you're lucky. Things have changed so much that your prior experience may not have much relationship to the process today. You can start fresh in the buying process, armed with the information presented in this book.

Buying a home is a big decision. For many, it is the largest investment they'll ever make in their lives. That's why doing it the *right* way is so important. In this book, I'll provide you a specific, well-thought-out process for buying a home. I created my version of this process to help buyers avoid some of the mistakes I saw buyers make in my two decades as a real estate agent and manager. Even though buying a home entails spending more dollars than most people ever spend for anything else, buyers go about buying a home with less forethought than they use to choose a place to have dinner!

Both first-time and repeat buyers can profit from this book. I'll explain my version of the buying process, and how you can use it to stay in control in each part of the process. Since almost all buyers use a real estate agent when they buy, I'll give you lots of advice on how to choose a competent agent. In my opinion, choosing a good agent is the most important decision you'll make in buying a home. Most buyers, though, aren't choosy enough about a real estate agent, and that mistake costs them time and money.

So you'll be prepared to handle all the phases of the buying process, I've included some "insider secrets," perspectives gained from my two decades inside the real estate business. Knowing these secrets will help you make good decisions and enable you to get back on track if you veer temporarily off course.

The Information Explosion: Good News for Buyers?

One of the biggest differences between buying a home today and buying five years ago is the buyer's ability to get information that was formerly unavailable or denied to him. In the past, the only way to find information on a community, view available properties, and learn about schools and amenities was to contact a real estate company that specialized in relocating buyers and sellers in the area where you were moving. You would have asked for a relocation kit—and waited a week or two to get it. Today, you can "surf the Net" and find this information immediately and shop for real estate agents and loan rates in the bargain! (You'll see some of those sources in this book's "Other Helpful Sources" section.)

Sound like all the information you need to purchase a home is right at your fingertips? Not so fast.

Sorting It All Out

Today, the breadth of information at a homebuyer's fingertips is awesome. Indeed, the wealth of information creates a new problem: How to prioritize it! It's like going to the library to check out four books on buying a home, and finding that 25 books are available. My job, in this book, is to help you sift through this information.

Who's the expert?   Because there's so much information about *everything* available today, most of us will not attempt to prioritize it ourselves unless we know a lot about the topic. We'll try to find someone to trust—an "expert" to help us prioritize it. That can be just as difficult a proposition as sorting all the information ourselves.

In a recent Phi Beta Kappa newsletter, Gertrude Himmelfarb, professor emeritus of history at the Graduate School of the City University of New York, points out that the information revolution has given us all access to much more information than ever before. That's the good news. However, cyberspace has made it seem that every source is as authoritative as every other. She mentions a ten-year old child who said it was great to be able to ask a question on a home page and get the answer from lots of people. Okay maybe for the ten-year old. But, when you're buying a home, you don't want to rely on just anyone for advice that affects your life. We have to decide whose information to trust.

If you're like most buyers, you'll be relying on a real estate agent for much of your purchasing information and guidance. That's why I believe the choice of a particular agent is the most important buying decision you'll make. It makes sense to choose an agent who can give you expert advice. I'll give you guidelines to ensure that you get trustworthy, prioritized information from a competent agent.

The Real Estate Revolution

It might be the quietest revolution going on today. Some inside the real estate industry wouldn't even call it a revolution, merely an evolution. Not me. Having been in the real estate business for over two decades, I see tremendous changes occurring right now, changes that are dramatically remolding the face of the industry. These changes greatly impact you as a buyer. As you go through the buying process, you'll see evidence of these changes. Armed with the information and the insider secrets here presented in this book, you'll be able to react to situations created by these changes and stay in control of your buying process.

Seven Trends That Influence Your Buying Experience

Among the many changes in the real estate industry, seven directly affect your buying experience—and ensure it will be different from before:

1. Real estate company profits are plummeting.

2. More operating costs are being passed on to the agent.
3. Affinity businesses are capturing commission dollars.
4. Big companies are getting bigger.
5. Offices are shrinking—or expanding—dramatically.
6. Fewer agents are entering the business.
7. More agents are representing buyers.

Let's look at each of these and what they mean to you.

1. Real estate company profits are plummeting.

Expenses of real estate companies have escalated while profits have shrunk dramatically. This situation has caused companies to make changes to protect their profit pictures. Most of these solutions, so far, have focused on short-term fixes—tactics that cut expenses. A case in point: Owners of companies say that their biggest problem is that many of their agents aren't productive enough. You might guess owners would terminate those agents or put them into production-producing sales programs. Not so. Here's the solution many cost-cutting owners have come up with: They've assigned low-producing agents to share desks. In the short term, this works to increase the bottom line, because owners can reduce the expense per agent. However, it also increases the chances that you could get a low-producing or part-time agent when you deal with that company. Is that good for you? No.

If this kind of a move to get more profits is not good for the buyer, why do owners make this move? These owners need the money *now*. They have decided that any commissions generated in any way from any type of agent are better than none. These owners are not concerned with the kind of buying experience you will have with one of their low-producing agents, but *you* should be. These developments make it even more important that you choose your real estate agent carefully. If you take whatever you get, you have more chances than ever to work with a part-timer or a low producer.

2. More operating costs are being passed on to the agent.

Almost all real estate agents are paid on a commission basis. Very few get a salary or a draw.

Agents earn commissions two ways:

1. When they sell a home
2. When a home they have listed for sale is sold (That means they contract with a seller to market the property to other agents;

then, when any agent sells the property, the "listing agent," the person representing the seller and marketing the property, shares the total commission with the selling agent.)

By law, all commissions must be paid to the agent's company first. Then, they are divided between the agent and the company, according to prior agreement. Being an agent can be expensive and risky. Even if the agent is earning no commissions, the agent has operating expenses to pay—hundreds to thousands of dollars per month.

Until about 15 years ago, the company and the agent generally split the commissions from listings and sales generated by an agent 50-50. In the industry, companies that offer this type of commission arrangement are called "traditional." Here's how the arrangement works. If the commission that came to the company as a result of an agent's sale was $4,000, the company got $2,000 and the agent got $2,000. That gave the owner lots of operating capital, money he could spend on providing agents the services they needed and generating reasonable profits.

Then some companies started offering more generous commission arrangements that wooed agents from traditional companies to these new ones. Where the agent had once received half of the total commission dollars that came into the company when the agent's listing sold, now, in these new companies, the agent could receive 60 to 90 percent. I'll show you how this would work. Let's say the agent was on a 75 percent split, with the company receiving 25 percent of the total commission. So, if a total commission on a sale was $4,000, the agent got $3,000, and the company got $1,000. As you can imagine, agents ran for the exits to join the companies with the more generous commission splits. Then, owners in traditional 50-50 companies found they had to give their agents more of the total commissions to match those of the more generous companies—or lose the agents.

Besides the variable commission splits I've mentioned, there's another method of paying agents—the 100 percent concept. In this arrangement, the agent receives all of the commission dollars that come into the company, but he pays a fee for a desk space, which can range from $300 to $2,000. That's how the 100 percent company makes its money. In this kind of arrangement, the agent also pays for all his office expenses, which can run from $500 to $2,000 per month. In this arrangement, the agent is truly in business for himself, with all the responsibilities the business owner has of allocating his dollars wisely to run his business successfully.

Giving the agents more of the commission dollars in the traditional companies obviously reduced owners' profits. These profits have continued downward as a result of higher agent commissions and increased operating costs. Although agents got more of the commission dollars, they wanted the same level of services from owners as they had on a 50-50 split. Owners knew that wasn't possible with their profit picture. So, to get back some of the commission dollars and provide services, owners have charged agents for various operating costs, including marketing, secretarial services, and phone calls. Now, even though the agent gets a healthy commission when he sells a home, the agent must pay many of his own operating costs. In fact, an agent's business expenses can easily run 20 to 40 percent of his gross commissions, or $300 to $1,000 per month.

Even though agents are capturing more of the commission dollars, many find it difficult to manage their businesses financially, because they have little experience as business owners. So, when you choose an agent, you'll want one who is good at managing his expenses and investing back into his business. You'll expect your agent to invest in the technology, education, and training needed to serve you properly. You don't want an agent whose motto is, "I'll sell three homes this year and avoid spending any money on operating costs"—a mentality of many low-producing agents. My questionnaire for choosing your real estate agent will guard you from getting a penny-pinching low producer.

3. Affinity businesses are capturing some of the commission dollars.   Not only are a owner's costs escalating while his profits go down—other businesses want a piece of the commission pie. These businesses, which can provide services to real estate companies for mutual benefit, form "affinity relationships" to trade business opportunities. These arrangements supposedly benefit both real estate company and cooperating company. Buyers can benefit, too, from these affinity relationships, but there are some dangers, as I'll explain here.

Referrals are a good example of how these affinity relationships operate. Companies such as Costco and Amway have formed referral relationships with large real estate companies. In return for referring members to the real estate company, Costco and Amway are paid a referral fee. These fees typically are 30 to 40 percent of the commissions earned by the company on a particular transaction. Some of that fee goes back to the Costco or Amway customer. Sounds like a super deal for a real estate company, doesn't it? For only 35 percent reduction of the normal commission, owners get hundreds, even thousands of sales leads.

Is this good for you? Not necessarily. You may be referred to an agent who has nothing better to do than sit around and wait for one of these leads to be handed to him. This agent is willing to work for less, but not willing to do *much* work for less. You, then, are the lucky recipient of this attitude. In this book are tips on what to do if you get a match-up that's not made in heaven.

Another type of affiliation real estate companies have formed is with businesses that complete the real estate transaction: Mortgage, title, inspection, and closing companies and attorneys, for instance. These are all businesses whose jobs are to see that the home you are buying actually becomes yours legally. Sometimes real estate companies even own these entities. The goal of these affiliations is to provide a seamless real estate transaction experience, what they like to call a "one-stop" homebuying experience. It sounds like a wonderful idea, but, since so much of your experience with your real estate transaction depends on the individuals involved in it, it's a little more difficult to execute a quality one-stop experience than you'd imagine. When you get a "package," or a one-stop transaction, you're less able to pick the players.

If you're working with an agent who suggests you use certain mortgage, title, inspection, and closing companies (or combination of them), find out who owns what, and how working with this group of affiliated businesses is in your best interests. This trend toward one-stops will continue, so your chances of becoming involved in such an arrangement will increase.

4. Big companies are getting bigger. As profits shrink and commission dollars are funneled off to affinity relationships, owners struggle to stay afloat, much less prosper. One solution for owners has been to stampede toward the franchise. They seem to believe there's safety in numbers, and they also want the business support that a franchise's corporate services can provide. The result of this stampede is that midsize companies have found it hard to survive independently, for name recognition in this era of information overload has become increasingly important.

What does this mean to you? Your chances of working with an agent who is affiliated with a franchise name are one in three. Does this mean your favorite franchise can supply you with any number of high-quality agents? No. Does this mean you could work with any agent in a particular franchise and get the same level of service? No. Real estate franchises don't exert quality control like a McDonald's or a Nordstrom. It's much harder to ensure a certain level of agent-customer service than it is to ensure that a product is consistent from franchise to franchise. As you'll see in this book, it's dangerous to rely on a company or franchise name to provide you with a competent agent every time. Instead, you'll need to choose your agent carefully, and look for the back-up of a good company name, regardless of whether the company is affiliated with a franchise.

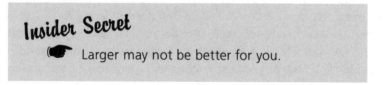

Insider Secret

☞ Larger may not be better for you.

The large company.   Buyers frequently are drawn to the large company or office simply because they've heard of it. But, is it necessarily a better choice? No. According to the NAR, large offices usually have more part-timers, more new agents, and more turnover. None of these situations is good for you. Remember, you're not going to be working with a whole office. You'll be working with one agent. Don't assume that because the office or company is large or well known in the area you'll automatically get a competent agent. Of course, many wonderful agents work in large offices and companies. I've worked with many of them, and I managed two large offices in large companies. But I would never walk into a real estate office I'd heard of and take any agent they gave me. Screening your agent carefully is critical to a pleasant buying experience.

The small company.   If more and more companies are joining franchises, and midsize companies are disappearing, what's happening to the small, independent company? First, what's small? The NAR categorizes firms with fewer than five agents as small. These real estate companies still account for 90 percent of companies in the U.S.; however, they account for just 5 percent of the sales force.

If these small companies are good at what they do, and many of them are excellent, they are thriving in this changing real estate environment. You'll find some of the best smaller, independent companies in midsize cities or small communities. When you're looking for an agent and you hear an agent's name mentioned more than once but don't recognize the company, please don't cross that agent off your list. Remember, you're picking the agent whose level of service will meet your expectations. The company name is secondary.

5. Offices are shrinking—or expanding—dramatically. When you bought your last home, chances are your agent had a desk at the real estate office. She didn't work out of her home. That's changed, and technology has been the driving force. Agents can sit at home and get information about newly listed properties from their multiple listing service (MLS), the service that gathers, organizes, and disseminates information about properties listed by MLS members. They can also communicate with their real estate offices, other agents, retrieve mortgage and property information, and even qualify buyers financially via computer.

As technology has changed the way agents work, it's also changed the way a real estate office looks. At any given time, owners know that no more than about 20 percent of their agents will be in the office. So, owners reason, why have all that expensive office space? Why have a desk for every agent, if they're working from their homes? So, owners are reducing the amount of office space. Some have even created what they call a virtual office—a large space for technology, a couple of conference rooms, a manager's office, and a few desks that agents can use when they come into the office. Don't be surprised when you walk into a real estate office and find out it's shrunk from your last buying experience.

What does this mean to you? That it may be more difficult than it was previously to get in touch with a real estate salesperson when you need to, since so many are working from their homes. Agents want their calls to come directly to them, so they have their own phone numbers. Many times those private lines ring into their homes. Although agents may want to be responsive to calls, they simply aren't as reliable as the hired office receptionist. (Career-oriented agents complain regularly about how difficult it is to track down other agents today.) In fact, when you call an agent on her own business line, you may be surprised how many times the agent's receptionist sounds as if she's about six years old. She is. It's the agent's daughter.

Real Life

Up to this point in the book, I've spoken of company owners and real estate agents. Before we go further, I need to introduce two more functions in a real estate company that use real estate specific terms. Those are the *broker* and the *manager*. Let's look first at what a broker is and the several ways the term can be used.

Who can become a real estate broker? A real estate licensee who has been in the business a few years (generally two), takes a certain number of prescribed real estate courses, and passes the broker licensing exam. The licensee must pay a fee and tell his state licensing department how he wishes to use his new broker's license. The type of broker's license the licensee gets depends on the job function he has with his company. Here are the various functions:

- *Managing an office.* If the licensee with the broker's license is managing an office, he is termed a "managing broker." (All managers must have broker's licenses). In some areas of the country, we call the manager of an office simply the "manager." If there are several branch offices in the company, the manager may be called a "branch manager." In this book, I'll call those who manage offices "managers." In smaller companies, the manager is also the owner of the office.
- *Selling real estate.* If the licensee who has gained a broker's license is selling real estate, not managing, he will be licensed as a associate broker. (You will probably see that designation on business cards of some of the salespeople you meet.)

- *Designated as responsible for all licensees in the firm.* The person who is legally responsible for the lawful activities of the licensed agents in a firm is termed the "designated broker." He may be the owner or someone else in the firm with a broker's license. There's only one designated broker per firm. As a consumer, you probably won't be talking with the designated broker unless you are working with a small company, where the owner is the manager and is the designated broker. Or, you may have a complaint with a large company that you take to the top, by calling the designated broker. In a large company, the designated broker generally does not manage an office.

Insider Secret

☛ You may know more agents in an office than their own manager recognizes.

The incredible expanding office. While some owners have tried to solve their profit problems by shrinking their offices, others have done the opposite. They've reasoned that they can cut their costs and multiply their profits by putting hundreds of desks in one office. In metropolitan areas, it's common to find two or three of these "megaoffices," with 150 to 200 agents in one place. With that many agents, it's difficult for the manager to keep track of who these people are—much less what they're doing!

Agents in these megaoffices capture 100 percent of the total commissions paid into the company. The company makes its money by charging the agent a fee for a desk, and for any expenses incurred by the agent. The megaoffice attracts agents by offering inexpensive desk rents. For $300 to $800 per month, an agent can hang her license in the office and rent office space from the company. In these arrangements, the agent pays for every service, from copies to faxes. The more business she does, the more it costs her. It's a haven for the part-timer, because she can operate inexpensively with little responsibility to the company—and little supervision. She has no obligation to the owner of the company to sell a certain number of properties, because the owner is not paid through the agent's commissions. So, there are generally no production standards. In this company's structure, there's only one entry requirement: If an agent can pay the desk fee, she can join.

What does this arrangement mean to you? With no hiring guidelines from the owner, you can imagine that the kind of agent in the megaoffice can range from very good to never there, from ethical practitioner to questionable. Most are part-timers. Many are semiretired from the real estate business, selling three to four homes a year. If you are thinking about working with an agent from a megaoffice, be sure to interview that agent using the qualifying guidelines outlined in Chapter 3. You want a career-oriented, energetic agent with current, ethical business practices, who will devote enough time to you to ensure you get what you want.

Standards are hard to enforce.   Agents working from home and megaoffices make it difficult for brokers to set and enforce standards. These trends are driven by the owners' need for short-term profits. Trying to control how an agent works with buyers means that the broker must be willing to try to correct an agent's behavior—and be willing to lose the agent to another company. The motto of some agents is, "The ends justify the means." When a manager tells an agent that she can't operate the way she has been operating, the agent just takes her license down the street. Some other manager will hire her, no matter what she's done, because some managers are desperate for anyone with a real estate license.

In many companies, the standards of performance expected from the agent are down to one or two: "Can you pay me my desk fee per month, and avoid getting us sued?" As you can see, these standards have nothing to do with how the agent does her business (except to avoid lawsuits). If you have a complaint about how you've been treated, and you're dealing with one of these companies, don't expect much. In a few companies, though, there are standards of performance measured by how satisfied the customer is with the experience. Obviously, this is the kind of agent and company you want to work with. If you have a complaint with this company (and the chances are far less you will), you'll find the manager and agent receptive to your concerns, and anxious to make it right with you. The information in Chapter 3 will help you identify agents and companies who care about providing top-level customer service.

6. Fewer agents are entering the business.

The number of real estate agents entering the business has dwindled in the last few years. This is due to increasingly higher educational standards required to get a license, and much greater financial commitment needed to get started. Today, on average, to get a real estate license, an agent must complete about 60 hours of study (some states require less, and some require 120 or more hours). Managers tell prospective agents that it will cost them $1,000 to 2,000 to enter the business; they recommend that new agents have six months living expenses set aside. As you can see, these requirements narrow the field of potential entrants.

At the other end of the spectrum, experienced agents are getting out of the business. To be successful today, the agent must run his business like a business. He must invest in technology and personal marketing. For many experienced agents, this change in business requirements has come as a shock. They were used to investing nothing or very little. Buying their own equipment, especially a laptop computer, even five years ago, was exceptional. Now, it's becoming a necessity. Instead of investing in new equipment and education, many experienced agents are simply quitting, and this trend will escalate. It's predicted that within five years, most of these resistant experienced agents will be gone, replaced with techno-savvy, committed careerists. According to data from the NAR, we will see a reduction in REALTOR® members, from a total in 1996 of 700,000, to about 400,000 by the year 2000. As you can imagine, the number of part-timers is dwindling too. The good news for you is that, as we near the year 2000, low-producing, noncommitted agents will find it increasingly difficult to pick off a sale once in a while. You can do your part, too, by choosing your agent carefully, avoiding those low producers and part-timers.

Insider Secret

☛ The next time you visit the real estate office, you'll see a whole sea of new faces.

Real estate salespeople are a transient bunch.
It's been a year since you bought your home, and you've decided to
drop into the real estate office and see your agent. Since you spent a few
hours in the office last year, you got to know quite a few of the agents.
Now, as you look around the office, you see many new faces. What's
going on? The same thing that happens in most real estate offices.
About 20 percent of agents are new to the office each year! Your
chances are one out of five that the agent is rather new to the office (not
necessarily new to the business). So, don't rely on the brand name of
an office or company to choose an agent. With so many agents getting
out of the business, you could be working with an agent who won't be
there for the end of your transaction.

Insider Secret

☞ Just because your agent is driving a Mercedes, doesn't mean she can make the house payment.

Signs of success.   How much money do you think the average
REALTOR® makes a year? The NAR asked that question, and found that
the consumer thought a REALTOR® made, on average, $50,000 a year.
Halve that figure, and you're about right. In 1995, gross median income
for a nonbroker REALTOR® (one half made more, one half less) was
$26,400, and net income was $17,700. Agents with brokers' licenses
(associate brokers) did better, grossing $48,000 and netting about
$38,000. For either agents or associate brokers, that's not enough
income to drive a Mercedes and make a house payment.

How do agents support themselves with this level of income? Studies by the NAR have shown that many REALTORS® have other sources
of income, and don't rely solely on their real estate sales income to support themselves. Beware: The agent you choose may not be what she
appears. In Chapter 3, I'll give you some questions you can ask to find
out whether the agent is doing enough business selling homes to be
good at it.

7. More agents are representing buyers.

Historically, the real estate industry has focused on meeting the needs of sellers. In fact, until a few years ago, all agents legally could represent only sellers. Sellers were the agents' clients. Now, agents are also representing buyers. This is called "buyer representation" or "buyer agency." A buyer represented by an agent is his client, just like a seller represented by an agent is *his* client.

In the last few years, many real estate professionals have started specializing in working with buyers. Agents have started treating buyers' needs as carefully as they have always treated sellers' needs. They've designed the same types of marketing and consulting programs for buyers as they had previously created only for sellers. Some have even decided to become buyers' specialists. A few have taken specializing with buyers even further. They call themselves "exclusive buyer representatives," and they do not represent sellers at all (that is, they do not list properties; they only sell properties as buyer representatives).

In the past, almost all agents represented sellers, even if they were helping buyers find homes. In Chapter 4, I'll explain in depth the concept of buyer representation and how it affects your buying process. For now, I want to point out that this development is positive for buyers, for you have the same level of representation and services available that had previously been offered to sellers.

Out of Chaos, What Will Emerge?

For the past three years, I've been a speaker at national real estate brokers' conferences, where managers and owners from all over the United States come to discuss challenges, trends, and possible solutions. As I walk away from those conferences I sense many managers and owners truly don't know which direction to take to ensure they'll be in business three years from now. Some of them are sold on the solutions I've noted in this chapter, solutions that can deliver short-term profits, but at the buyer's expense. Others, though, are finding solutions that not only ensure long-term profits, but also ensure you'll have a good buying experience. These solutions are the same that great service businesses in other fields have found are key to providing high levels of customer satisfaction, which, in turn, ensure long-term profits:

- Focus on the quality of the associates they hire, armed with solid values and guidelines.
- Focus on satisfying consumer needs, aiming for stunning customer satisfaction. (Think Nordstrom.)

These solutions for profits are in your best interests. The other solutions owners have implemented, listed earlier, are not. As you start your buying process, look for the real estate agent and company that most epitomizes these concepts. You'll get the best service, the best experience, and you'll find a long-term business relationship you can count on when you need real estate advice. Why settle for less?

As you walk into a real estate office today, you won't see any chaos. You won't see a "revolution." It's all happening behind the scenes. I've listed the changes and trends that are causing so much uncertainty inside the industry. I've described the solutions owners are implementing that impact your buying process. You'll start experiencing how these changes affect you as you get into your buying process. Armed with the insider secrets in this book, you'll be in control of any situation. Now, let's start your buying process.

Frequently Asked Questions

Q. You said that part-timers and low-producing agents will have to get out of the business. Yet, you warned against working with these types of agents now. If they're getting out, why should I be concerned that I might find one?

A. Because the business hasn't cleaned house yet. Owners are still keeping low producers and part-timers. They are cutting their operating costs by having them share a desk, or by sending them home. It will take a few more years before the industry has a majority of good producers.

Q. There are three large companies in our area. I've heard they're all good. How do I choose the best?

A. Never choose a company and take whatever agent you get. All companies have a variety of agents (some have a greater variety than others!). Think of it this way: Your buying experience will be dependent not on a real estate company, but on an individual agent. You'll be relying on the judgments, ethics, and hard work the agent uses—or doesn't.

Q. Do you mean, then, that the company isn't important at all?

A. No. If you're trying to decide between two agents and one is with a company whose name you believe is reputable, and one is with a company whose name isn't so good, of course, choose the agent with the reputable company.

Q. A company in my area advertises that it is "number one in service," and that it is "number one in sales in the area." Isn't that my best choice?

A. Let me ask you: Who says? Don't take those slogans seriously. Real estate companies—and agents—love those "jingles." However, they may not be backed up by statistics (or the statistics are really suspect). There's a big difference between reputable and big. Can you have both? Yes, and you can have one without the other. Remember, choose the agent, backed by a reputable company.

2

Starting the Homebuying Search the Right Way

*M*ost homebuyers start the process of homebuying by looking at properties. Buyers want to get a "feel" of the areas and properties they may want to buy. If you're like most buyers, you'll probably drive around areas where you may want to consider living. You'll stop into open houses. You may call on some ads, just to see where the properties are located. Now, it's okay to get some background education that way. But, stop there. Don't zero in on your home search and find the home of your dreams, without first choosing your real estate agent. That's the biggest mistake buyers make in the whole buying process. They focus on finding a *property,* not finding an *agent.* They look on their own for properties, find one, and buy it from whatever real estate licensee is available. They don't know they need an agent who's right for them. They think all agents are alike. When a buyer chooses a home and lets any agent sell it to him, that buyer is asking for trouble. Real estate agents can range from the consummate professional to the incompetent—or untrustworthy.

Since almost 90 percent of buyers use the assistance of a real estate agent in purchasing a home, chances are you'll be working with an agent, too, at some point. To avoid living a homebuying horror story, and ensure you have a pleasant buying experience, do two things:

1. Make choosing the agent as important as choosing the property.

2. Choose your real estate agent very early in your buying process.

You may wonder why I'm stressing the importance of *choosing* a real estate agent. After all, those authorized to sell real estate are *licensed* by the state, aren't they? True, but in most states, it is very easy to get a real estate license. Although some states require a certain number of hours of study (from 10 to 90), some don't. All require passing a state exam of about 100 multiple-choice questions. The exam has no questions on it about customer service, ethics, or communication—issues that affect the sales competency of an agent. Exams deal only with real estate laws and regulations. After passing the exam, the applicant has only two moves to make to get a license. He must send a completed application to the state, with a signature from the owner (or his designated representative) of the company who will be contracting with him. (Agents are normally not employees. They are independent contractors.) He must pay a fee of about $75, depending on the state. In many states, it's much more difficult to get a beautician's license than a real estate license! That's why it's so important that you create your own "exam," a list of questions like those I've supplied in this chapter and in Chapter 3, to qualify and choose an agent you believe will meet your needs.

In this chapter, I'll outline my version of the entire buying process. Then, I'll identify sources for potential good agents, since choosing an agent is an important early step in your buying process. I'll tell you which sources are better, and how to screen candidates in each source. I'll also give you tips and insider secrets of what to watch out for as you investigate these sources. Please note that I've tried to avoid using the term "your agent" because it has certain legal implications. To be precise, an agent isn't *your* agent unless she is representing you. Then, she is termed a "buyer's agent." However, it's common to call an agent working with you, the buyer, *your* agent, whether or not you're legally represented by her. The issue of representation will be fully explored in Chapter 4.

The Buying Process: My Version

Let's first look at the process as a whole. I'll explain what each part of the process entails. Later chapters of this book will go into each step in detail. Figure 2.1 shows you a flowchart of the nine steps you should

FIGURE 2.1 • **Your Steps in Purchasing a Home**

Action	Time Frame	Professionals
1. Research properties; locate agent candidates.	Days to weeks	
2. Hold a consultation meeting with agent.	Before looking for homes in earnest	Real estate agent
3. Apply to get preapproved for a loan.	Week one	Loan officer
Agent prepares home tour.		Real estate agent
4. Buyer and agent view homes and prioritize homes viewed.	Week one+	Real estate agent
5. Buyer makes purchasing decision; agreement is negotiated.	Takes 1 to 14 days	Buyer's agent Listing agent
6. Buyer continues loan process; escrow is opened.	30 days, on average for approval	Loan officer Loan processor Escrow officer Loan underwriter Attorney
7. Property inspected; conditions on agreement satisfied.	3 to 30 days	Home inspector Pest inspector Others, according to agreement
8. Loan approved.	30 days from application	Mortgage company
9. Loan closes; buyer gets possession (according to agreement) or "passes papers."	30 to 45 days from agreement	Closing entity

take through the process—and the order in which you should take them.

1. Identifying Candidates for Agent of Your Choice

If you're like most buyers, you'll be casually looking at properties for a while before you get serious about purchasing a home. At the same time as you're researching properties, you're liable to start working with a real estate agent—without consciously choosing that agent as your best choice. Let's say you're visiting an open house on Sunday. You start talking with the agent, and the agent tells you about other properties available. She makes an appointment with you to see these other properties. Before you know it, you're seeing properties every week with that agent. How did you choose that agent? Not very carefully, just casually. That's not good enough. In this chapter, I'll tell you how to sort through your sources for agents, choose good agent candidates, and get your buying process started right.

2. The Consultation

You are researching properties to get background information on purchasing a home. Although that is a buyer's first step, it is not a formal part of the buying process. The first real formal, or organized step of the process is the consultation. This is sometimes called the "qualifying" or "interview" session. What is a consultation? A one- to two-hour meeting with an agent, an agent you located, I hope, from one of the best sources named later in this chapter. The consultation should be the first "formal" step of the buying process. Many buyers don't ever take part in a consultation. Why? Two reasons:

1. They haven't chosen an agent who works as I recommend.
2. They don't realize they should start the formal part of the process with a consultation.

If buyers skip the consultation, they miss critical information they need to get the process started right. Here is the type of information you should gather from this consultation:

- Time frames involved in purchasing
- Area market trends and how they affect your buying decisions
- Benefits of buying versus renting

- Tax advantages of ownership/taxes in the area
- Costs of purchasing
- Financing alternatives
- School, community, and other amenities in areas of interest

The agent will ask you to describe what you want to buy. She will provide information about availability of the type of properties you find attractive. She'll provide you guidelines for financing and may ask you some financial questions, so both of you will know what price ranges you qualify for. She'll probably recommend three lending institutions and suggest that you call each, meet with the loan officers, and find out your buying perimeters (how much home you can buy), and which loan programs meet your needs. It's important that you get this information now, so you'll see the right homes when you and your agent start viewing properties in earnest.

At its best, the consultation is a mutual exchange of information. At the end of the consultation, you should have a good idea of how much home you can purchase, of whether the home you described actually exists in your price range, of how market trends will impact your buying decisions, and about buying practices in the area. You should have your specific questions answered to your satisfaction.

When to make the final choice of agent.   By the time you have a formal consultation, you may have already decided to work with this agent, because you've gotten to know the agent through one of the sources I've listed in this chapter. That's okay, as long as you have qualified the agent adequately using my quick qualifying questions in this chapter, and my larger questionnaire in Chapter 3. Usually, though, you will not have had the opportunity yet to adequately screen this agent. So, your job during this consultation is to screen the agent and make the final choice about whether to work with her.

During this consultation, you should be observing how the agent works. You'll have the opportunity to ask her your qualifying questions. At the end of this consultation, you should decide whether you want to work with this agent. The agent, in turn, should have a good idea of whether you are realistic about purchasing a home, whether you are a serious buyer, and whether you will be able to get a commitment for a home loan. The agent, too, will be making a decision about whether to work with you. You are evaluating each other, both deciding if you want to work together. Starting right with a good consultation is key to having a pleasant buying experience. It makes finding the right property for you much easier.

3. Meeting with the Loan Officer

After meeting with the agent, you should get all the information on various loan programs from a loan officer. You may have done this prior to meeting with the agent, which is okay. Besides getting information, you will also get an idea of the amount of mortgage a loan company will provide. You may even go through the formal process of obtaining a loan commitment from a loan company.

In general, this formal approval process is called "qualifying" for a loan. That is, at some point prior to finalizing the purchase on a home, you get a written commitment from an entity that makes mortgages (a bank, a savings and loan company, or a mortgage company) that they will provide a mortgage for the amount you need to purchase the home. Here's what happens in the qualification process. You provide the loan company with all your financial information, which the loan company reviews. Applying its guidelines for making loans, it issues you a "letter of commitment." That means the loan company promises to provide a mortgage at a certain rate. Generally, it takes about 30 days to get a loan commitment.

There are two different methods buyers use to find out how large a loan commitment they qualify for. The first is an informal process. The buyer meets with a loan officer, and the loan officer asks questions about the buyer's financial situation. Based on the buyer's answers (with no substantiation or further research), the loan officer tells the buyer the mortgage amount he qualifies for. There is no formal commitment from the loan officer. The buyer is then "prequalified." Although this informal process doesn't provide firm assurances that a buyer can obtain a certain mortgage, it does give him valuable information about various programs and an idea of the amount of mortgage.

The second method is a formal process in which the buyer goes through all the steps to get a written commitment for a loan prior to buying a home. The buyer who gets a commitment for a loan this way is called "preapproved." (If the buyer were to get a commitment for a loan after purchasing a home, he would be "approved.") When you are preapproved, you pay a credit report fee of about $100, fill out all the loan application forms, and go through the qualification process, just as you would if you had already purchased a home. Why go through all that before you purchase? For three reasons:

1. You'll know all the loan programs available, and will get the information from the best source, a good loan officer.
2. You'll be able to choose the best loan for you, without the pressure of having to make those decisions right after you've just purchased a home (and in a very short time frame).
3. You'll have a letter issued by the mortgage company saying you are qualified for a certain mortgage amount. You can use this letter to make your negotiation position more attractive to sellers (they'll know you can get financing for their home, if their house is appraised for what you offer to pay).

4. Finding, Viewing, and Prioritizing Your Home Choices

Now you have the information you need to start your home search. During the time you've been educated and prequalified or preapproved by your loan officer, the agent has been searching appropriate properties for you. Now, you meet, view the properties she has selected, and give the agent feedback. You probably will be viewing properties more than once. In fact, according to the NAR, buyers see 18 properties on average before making a buying decision. You'll probably view four or five in each viewing session.

5. Making Your Purchasing Decision and Negotiating to Agreement

Once you find the right property, you will write an offer to purchase (sometimes called a "purchase and sale agreement") by strategizing with the agent; then, the agent will present the offer to the seller, usually with the listing agent present. (Sometimes the listing agent presents the offer without the other agent present). If you're like most buyers, you'll be negotiating with the seller for a few days—through the agent with whom you're dealing. Finally, you and the seller will come to agreement, and the home will be considered by the real estate community a "pending sale." That is, although you and the seller have a completely signed offer, with both of you agreeing on all the terms and conditions of the sale, the home is not yet yours legally, because the final paperwork has not been completed.

6. Making Loan Application

Unless you're paying cash for the home (most buyers aren't), right after you've agreed with the seller on terms of the sale, you'll go back to the lending institution and formally apply for a loan. If you've been preapproved, much of this process has already been completed. Your offer to purchase will state how quickly you must make a loan application—and the amount of time you have to secure a loan for the property (if you must have a loan, which most buyers need).

7. Removing Any Contingencies in Your Offer

At the same time as you start the loan process, you may have some other work to get done besides financing to satisfy the terms of the offer. This other work may be in the form of "contingencies" you had placed in the offer. Contingencies are any clauses you put in the offer to give yourself an "out." Generally, contingencies will deal with questions you have about the property. You'll need to answer these questions to your satisfaction before you can make a final decision to purchase the property. A contingency says, in effect, that you must get the answer to a specific concern, to your satisfaction, to go ahead with the purchase. Both sellers and buyers may place contingencies in an offer.

Putting a contingency in a purchase and sale agreement allows you time to get information or an answer that you don't have when you first write the offer. For instance, a transferred buyer I worked with found a home he liked, but his wife was unable to see the property for several days. So, he bought the property "contingent on his wife's approval, within five days of mutual agreement." You guessed it. His wife flew to Seattle, looked at the property, and hated it! Because he had put in the "wife's inspection" contingency, he was able to get out of the offer and get his deposit back.

The most common contingency today is the inspection contingency. You'll want to make purchasing the home contingent on your approval of a home inspection (more about that in Chapter 9). If you buy a home built before 1978, you'll also need a contingency to assess lead paint hazards. It's the law that you have ten days to complete your assessment. Another type of contingency is placed in the offer when you have a home to sell. Since you must have the funds from that home to buy the new home, you must make your offer contingent upon sale of your first home. Because contingencies can become pretty complicated, you'll want to be working with a competent agent who can explain the ins and outs. It will usually take you about 30 days to remove any contingencies you may have placed in the agreement (unless you have a home to sell; then you may need to make that contingency a longer one).

8. Loan Approval and Preparation for Finalization of Ownership Transfer

It takes 30 to 60 days to secure financing. During this time, the entity in charge (it could be a title company, escrow company, or attorney) has been readying all the paperwork to prepare the transfer of the property to you.

9. Ownership Transfer

In 30 to 60 days, generally, after you and the seller agreed on an offer, the home is yours. Here's how that happens. The entity preparing the paperwork will call you for an appointment. You'll come in, bring your money, and sign the papers to transfer ownership to you. This is called a "closing" or "passing papers." There is a specific date when ownership is recorded with the county in your name, and monetary proceeds from the sale are available to the seller. This is usually the date on which you can have possession (check your offer for the specific date on which you have the right to occupy the property). Depending on the area of the country, closing or passing papers can occur when you sign papers, or within a few days. Be sure to check these time frames with the escrow company and real estate agent. Many miscommunications can occur during this time, which could be avoided with a look at the closing and possession date on the offer, and better coordination between seller and buyer.

Where to Find Agents

Finding a competent agent should be high on your list to begin the homebuying process. But, where can you find candidates? I've divided sources into three categories: Least reliable, moderately reliable, and very reliable. Here are the least reliable sources:

- Calling on property advertising (in the newspaper or homes magazines, television advertising, or real estate signs on properties)
- Walking into a real estate office
- Attending public open houses
- Surfing the Internet

You won't think of these sources as sources of *agents*. You'll think of them as sources for *properties*. But, as I've stressed, buyers typically search for properties and get an agent by default. I'll discuss these property searches in the context of finding an agent. Why do I consider these sources less reliable than others? Because most buyers who find agents via these sources don't take the time to qualify the agent when they run into them while looking for properties. In this section, I'll tell you what to watch out for, and give you some quick qualifiers to sort the wheat from the chaff.

Here are my moderately reliable sources:

- Calling the real estate office manager
- Being referred through an affinity group

Why? Because, at least, you are not confusing searching for properties with searching for agents. You will tend to pay more attention to the agent you're given, especially armed with my candidate qualifying questions.

My best sources are:

- Getting a personal referral—a friend or relative
- Having personal experience—your having worked with the agent before

These sources allow you to investigate how the agent works. Remember, we behave in the future as we behaved in the past. With these sources, you don't have to rely on sales promises, just on observed and remembered behavior.

I'll start with the least reliable sources; then I'll give you a list of questions to ask an agent to qualify him when you meet him through these sources—if you're interested enough to qualify him.

Insider Secret

☛ Calling a real estate office about an advertised home may get you more (and less) than you bargained for.

Least Reliable Sources for Agents

Calling on advertised property. You're reading the Sunday paper, and you see a home advertised that catches your eye. As you read the ad, your imagination conjures up your dream home—and it seems like the right price and area. You can hardly believe it. So, you pick up the phone, dial the number, and listen as an agent answers. You start asking questions about the property and hear all the right answers. You're anxious to see the property before someone else buys it, so you make arrangements to meet the agent at the home. Miracle of all miracles, the property is everything you hoped it would be. You're ecstatic, and hurriedly make an offer on the property with that agent.

You're so excited about buying that property that choosing the agent is the last thing on your mind. That may be a very expensive mistake. For one thing, the agent who is "helping" you may very well be a poor producer or new agent assigned to be the "floor time" representative (the person assigned to answer phone inquiries from ads or real estate signs, and to greet walk-ins), while the higher producers are out selling or listing houses. To get top-flight service, you'll want to work with an agent who has been "practicing" selling. He's more apt to know the market, the trends, and the latest laws affecting buyers. Generally, poorer producing agents and new agents are the ones who opt for floor time. Why? They want a chance to get some leads.

At one real estate office I managed, I found many of the agents were experienced, but low producers who liked to have floor-time assignments because they figured it was an easy way to get leads. Although they "sat the floor" (Don't you love these insider phrases?), they didn't sell anyone anything. I couldn't figure out why. I had my secretary tracking calls, so I knew they were engaging in conversation with buyers. I saw buyers walk in during their floor assignments. I knew they were getting leads. From closely tracking these low producers' activities over a period of three months, I discovered that they just didn't want to help a buyer who was too demanding. If it was really easy to sell someone a home, they would do it. You don't want to get stuck with an agent like that. (I didn't, either. I had to terminate ten of these experienced, low producers to protect buyers from that kind of real estate "practice.")

If you want to see a property you've seen advertised, go ahead, but don't commit yourself to working with that agent further until you've qualified him.

Walking into a real estate office.   When you walk into a real estate office, either to get information about a particular home or about buying in general, you're usually assigned the floor agent. Remember, this agent may be a new agent, low producer, or part-timer. Do not agree to work with that agent unless you have qualified her.

When in the real estate office, observe agents at work on ad calls and walk-ins. You can make valuable judgments about agents during your time with them, if you observe how they work. On a floor call, determine the expertise the agent uses in questioning you. Does she ask good questions, or merely rattle off the home's features? Does she ask about your needs? Does she listen? If you don't want to see that property, how does she handle the situation? Does she seem prepared to answer your questions, or is she disorganized? Does she tell you who she represents? (For more information, see Chapter 4.) The same observations would apply to walk-ins, with the added benefit that you're able to observe the agent's appearance, organization, and demeanor.

Attending open houses.   The same principle applies to open houses that applies to ad calls and walk-ins. Choosing an agent because he "goes with the property" is not a good idea. Open houses are used by agents just like they use floor time—to get leads. Agents know it's very seldom someone will walk into an open house and buy it (that happened to me once in my eight-year selling career, and I held open houses at hundreds of properties). Chances are much greater that the potential buyer will not like the open house—the price is too high, or the rooms are too small, etc. However, the agent sees this situation as an opportunity to show this buyer other homes.

I'm not faulting the agent for wanting to find buyers in this fashion. I just want you to realize that you should qualify that agent before you look at other homes with him—and, of course, if you intend to purchase that particular home. Here's the good news about open houses: You, as a buyer, have a chance to observe this agent at work in an open house. How organized is he? What kinds of promotional materials does he have available? How does he greet you? How well does he listen? What kind of questions does he ask? Does he seem interested in you? Do you like his sales approach?

> **Insider Secret**
> ☞ Looking for an agent to represent you? You may not meet one if you're choosing an agent who holds an open house.

Some well-qualified agents don't hold homes open.

If you're thinking you can cruise the open houses on a Sunday, and see all the agents available to work for you, you might want to think again. If an agent is working *exclusively* as a buyer's agent, she will not represent sellers. That is, she won't be listing homes at all. So, she won't hold homes open, for that would be a conflict of interest. I believe you'll see exclusive buyer representation become more common in the future. (For more about buyer representation, see Chapter 4.) Just remember to find out who that agent represents. It's common that agents representing sellers hold homes open.

Also, many top agents just don't spend Saturdays or Sundays holding open houses. They get most of their business from referrals. Do I mean you can't run into a good agent holding a home open? No. Just remember to qualify that agent before you make commitments to see other homes with him.

Beware of the "property expert" sales spiel.

You may hear the following sales spiel as you answer on an ad or visit an open house. The agent is trying to impress you. She says she knows all the properties available, and implies that others don't. Balderdash! With the magic of technology, the ability of any agent to get property information has never been easier. Although "inventory knowledge" is important, good agents see only enough properties to stay educated. When they know your needs, they'll preview appropriate properties. Poor agents, on the other hand, spend their time looking at pretty homes, and they'll always turn out for lunch during those open houses for agents! What agents do with the property information, how they work with you, and how they handle their businesses are much more important determinants about whether you want to work with them than their ability to access property information—or rattle off descriptions of all the properties they've just seen.

Insider Secret

☞ "I know all the properties available" may mean the agent previews them all for a free lunch.

Surfing the Internet.   Thousands of agents and real estate companies now have home pages on the World Wide Web. The quality and usefulness of the information varies from terrific to terrible. Why do they put all this information on the Web? To entice you to call the agent or the office. How is it working? Agents and companies are getting less than 5 percent of their business from their Web sites. As buyers use the Internet to buy in general, and the real estate sites get better, the proportion of business from these sites will increase. Buyers will increasingly educate themselves about products and services offered by various real estate companies and agents. Then, they'll contact the agent and company who have been most helpful.

Some agents' home pages are just "brag sheets." Others, though, are full of valuable information about the community and its amenities, schools, and properties. There are good tips to buyers and sellers, and many link to other useful sites. I'll give you the same advice I've given about finding agents through ads and open houses: Qualify the agent before agreeing to meet or look at properties with him. That way, you'll be sure you're getting what you want in service.

FIGURE 2.2 • **Finding Good Agent Candidates:
Quick Qualifying Questionnaire**

Use this qualifying questionnaire to pick agent candidates as you do property searches.

1. Is selling residential real estate your full-time career?

2. How many houses did you sell last year?

3. How long have you specialized in residential real estate in this area?

4. Describe the work you do in our price range and area.

5. Tell us how you will work with us.

Qualifying Questions to Ask Agents

To screen agents you meet in the sources I've just mentioned I think you should get answers for five critical questions. The questions are listed in Figure 2.2; here's what you should look for in the answers:

1. Is selling residential real estate your full-time career? Listen to be sure the agent specializes in residential real estate. You want someone who sells houses for a living, not apartment buildings. Listen to see if this is the agent's full-time career. Ask additional questions if the agent's answers need more clarifying.

2. How many houses did you sell last year? You want someone successful; that means, at minimum, the agent sold at least six houses in that year.

3. How long have you specialized in residential real estate in this area? Be sure the agent has expertise and interest in the area where you want to purchase. That means he should have worked in the area at least six months.

4. Describe the work you do in our price range and area. Listen to be sure the agent zeros in on the area and price range you need. If the agent says, "I work anywhere with anybody," that agent may not be for you, for he may be trying to cover too much ground to know very much about specific areas.

5. Tell us how you will work with us. Listen as the agent describes the buying process, as she views it. Does it reflect what I'm advising in this book? If not, question her about the differences.

Throughout your qualifying process, judge the agent's communication skills, especially her listening skills. Ask yourself if you find the agent's personality the kind you'd enjoy working with.

What should you do with your qualifying information? If this agent seems a likely candidate for you, go ahead and make a consultation appointment. Then, you can complete the qualifying questionnaire in Chapter 3. Or, you can continue your qualifying process now with more of those qualifying questions. The important point is that you consciously qualify and choose your agent before getting too far into the buying process.

Insider Secret

☞ A recommendation from a manager could snag you a "secret agent."

More Reliable Sources for Agents

Calling the real estate office manager. You want someone who's at least moderately successful in the real estate business, and who's been in the business long enough for the ink on her license to dry. So, it may seem a good idea to call the manager in an office near where you want to look for homes and get a recommendation. But, wait. How are you sure the manager will pick the right agent for you? Remember, many offices have part-timers, low producers, and new agents. The manager you call may try to help his poor, underproducing agents by giving them referrals—yours included. The manager knows, too, if he provides agents business, the agents probably won't leave him.

Let's say you call this manager and ask for a recommendation. He suggests an agent who, he says, is very experienced, very professional. What do those words mean? The manager would like you to think those mean the agent has successfully sold real estate for a number of years. However, because managers generally have no minimum performance expectations, the word *professional* can mean something other than *successful*. You're thinking that an experienced, professional agent is one who's made, perhaps, at least $50,000 last year. The broker's thinking that an experienced, professional agent is that agent who dresses well and keeps the broker out of lawsuits. (Little chance of a lawsuit, too, if the agent sells only four homes a year.) In the business, we call this agent a "secret agent." She has a real estate license, she doesn't cause trouble, but the broker and clients never see her. No one has really figured out what these agents do all day, but they don't make money. To avoid getting a secret agent, define your terms and gather your qualifying questions before you ask the broker for a recommendation. You can use the five questions listed in the previous section, and can add questions from my questionnaire in Chapter 3.

Here's another suggestion from Karyn Sandbeck, one of my agent advisers, who represents buyers exclusively. To get a good agent, Karyn suggests you ask the manager for a recommendation of an agent who specializes in working with buyers. Then, ask the manager if that person works in your price range, and in the area where you want to buy. You're qualifying the agent and narrowing the field so you're sure you get an agent who knows how to find you what you want.

Insider Secret

☛ Buying a home through an affinity referral may not be worth the bucks you "save."

Being referred through an affinity group.   One of the hottest real estate trends today is forming affinity relationships, which we explored in Chapter 1. As a buyer, one of the most common you may encounter is the referral network. Let's say you're a member of a large credit union, Dollars 'R Us. You're being transferred to another city in your area and you noticed in your last Dollars 'R Us newsletter that your credit union has created a referral agreement with a large real estate company in the city where you're moving. If you work through your credit union, they'll find you an agent to help you search for homes. And, they'll give you a 10 percent rebate of the commission paid on the buying part of the transaction.

Sounds great, right? Not necessarily. As I told you in the first chapter, you may get referred to a low-producing agent who just likes to sit and wait for leads. The affinity referral has another significant downside—no incentive for the agent to work hard. After all, the agent receives about 20 percent less from selling you a home than when he sells a home to someone not referred in this manner. I've observed that good agents don't like leads with reduced commissions. In fact, a broker in a large company surveyed and found that over one-third of his agents refused affinity leads with reduced commissions. After all, if you're a successful, busy, sought-after agent, why should you replace your larger fee business with a reduced-fee lead?

What should you do to make sure you get a good agent if you are referred through an affinity relationship? Take your agent-qualifying criteria with you, and, as you meet with the agent, qualify the agent first, and refuse to work with a particular agent if you don't think that agent will work hard in your best interests. You will have a liaison within the referring network and within the real estate company (it may be the company's relocation department, or the manager of the office). If an agent isn't responsive to your phone calls and needs, contact your liaison immediately and demand another agent. It's your time, your money, and your right to reasonable service. By the way, affinity rebates are illegal in some states.

Most Reliable Sources

Getting a personal referral. The more you can find out about an agent's past behavior with buyers, the better your choice will be. The best source for this kind of information is the referral. It's that "networking" idea. Find others who have been happy with the service of a particular agent, and you'll probably have the same kind of experience if you work with that agent.

How can you find people who have just worked with competent agents as buyers? Ask your cohorts at work. Ask your friends. Inquire at your social clubs and house of worship. You'll hear a couple of agents' names mentioned time and time again. Put those names on your candidate list.

Talking to professionals in businesses affiliated to real estate is a great way to get referrals. Visit lending institutions, escrow companies, and title companies in the area where you want to buy. Because they work with agents every day, they'll really know the good, the bad, and the ugly. They'll be happy to refer you to agents they know are good. Describe the price range and area where you want to buy as you ask for names, so these professionals can zero in on your needs. Remember, the more specific you can be, the better your chances will be of finding the right agent.

When you get the name of an agent from any of these sources, ask some questions. My agent advisory panel suggests these:

- Would you use that same agent again? Why or why not?
- Did the agent return calls promptly?
- Did the agent have an assistant? What were his duties?
- Did the agent understand what you were looking for?
- Did the agent really listen to your concerns?

Having personal experience.   Even though this is one of my preferred sources, I caution against merely going back to the agent you used before just because you know the name. Maybe that agent has changed her business (for better or worse). Maybe that agent has gotten too busy to work with you. Maybe she's no longer working in your price range. To be sure that agent is still the one for you, ask the agent the appropriate qualifying questions. Then, you'll be sure you've made the right decision.

What to do with the referrals.   Call two or three of the agents you think, based on what your referral sources said, would be well qualified to work with you. Over the phone, ask the five quick qualifying questions in Figure 2.2. Then, pick one agent (if you like what you hear), and arrange to meet. There, you can finish your qualification and start the rest of the buying process.

If you're referred to several agents.   If you're choosing two or three agents to qualify further, you can easily control the situation. However, it's different if several referral sources have asked their favorite agents to get in touch with you. All of a sudden, you get phone calls from three agents, each assuming you're going to work with that agent. If that happens, simply explain that you are using a process to choose your agent, and that you'd like to ask the caller a few questions. Interview all three and choose your favorite.

There's one more referral situation that is really the most uncomfortable. That's when your boss refers you to his mother-in-law—and you don't want to work with her! What should you do? Explain that you're using a process to choose your agent. You'd be happy to interview the recommended agent, as you'll be interviewing several. In the end, let's face it, sometimes, we'll have to work with that mother-in-law to keep our job!

The Reality: Buyers' Habits

I wish that all buyers would take my recommendations and pick agents from their most reliable sources. Or, at least, that they would qualify candidates they find from the least reliable sources. How are buyers choosing their real estate agents today? Figure 2.3 is from a study by the NAR on how buyers picked an agent. You'll see that about 60 percent of the time buyers did choose an agent to whom they had been referred or whom they knew or had worked with. Good work. That's the right way to do it. Choosing an agent based on how he has acted with buyers in prior transactions is the best way for you to predict the level of service you'll get.

What about the rest of the buyers? About 40 percent chose an agent pretty much by default. They were searching for properties and got an agent in the process. They walked into an office and met the floor person (the agent on duty). Or, they met the agent at an open house, met the agent at a builder's sales office, or called the number on an ad or sign and continued to work with that agent. That wouldn't be so bad if they had used some qualifying criteria. My experience, though, is that they don't. Most of the time, they didn't even realize they were picking an agent—or that they should be more careful in choosing an agent. They just worked with whoever was available from that contact. Generally, this is the group of buyers who are dissatisfied with the level of service they get. Be sure you're in the driver's seat by choosing your agent from your best sources. In the next chapter, we'll develop more specific criteria to help you make that choice.

FIGURE 2.3 • **How Buyers First Came into Contact with Real Estate Professional Who Assisted Them**

	All Buyers	First-time Buyer	Repeat Buyer	New Home-buyer	Existing Home-buyer
Walked into office and met sales agent on duty	7%	8%	6%	6%	7%
Met real estate agent at an open house	8	8	9	11	8
Met real estate agent at builder's sales office	2	1	2	10	*
Phoned real estate firm in reference to newspaper ad	11	16	9	8	12
Phoned real estate firm in reference to yard sign	9	10	8	4	10
Used that real estate agent before	7	2	10	7	7
Real estate agent was friend/neighbor/relative	19	19	18	17	19
Real estate agent was referred by friend/neighbor/relative	29	29	29	27	29
Other	8	6	10	11	8

*Less than one percent

Frequently Asked Questions

Q. I feel uncomfortable "grilling" a real estate agent. How can I open the conversation to ask those quick qualifying questions?

A. Start with, "I'm curious. How did you get into the real estate business?" Then, move into your first qualifying question. You'll naturally get the agent talking about his career; and, agents *love* to talk!

Q. I avoided making any commitments when I visited open houses last Sunday. But, now, agents I met at those open houses are calling me. I don't know what to say.

A. Just start asking your qualifying questions, and you'll be in the driver's seat. Remember, you have the right to choose the agent you want.

Q. I got three agent referrals from fellow employees at my business. I chose one. Should I tell my business associates who I didn't choose?

A. Yes. Simply thank each for his referral, and tell him that you chose an agent who you thought would be the "best match" for you.

3

Choosing the Right Agent for You

I hope I've persuaded you to put as much emphasis on choosing your agent as you will on choosing your property. In this chapter, I'll identify the qualities and skills buyers need in their agent of choice. I'll provide a qualifying questionnaire to give you in-depth information you need from an agent to make a good decision. Along the way, I'll dispel some myths about choosing an agent, along with dispensing some insider secrets.

What Buyers Want in a Real Estate Agent

According to a recent survey by the National Association of REALTORS® (NAR), consumers wanted three qualities in a real estate salesperson: Enthusiasm, knowledge, and honesty. The first two of these are relatively easy to observe in an agent. You can observe an agent's level of enthusiasm as you visit open houses. If the agent says to you as she lounges on the couch, "Just come in and look around. If you have any questions, ask me," you can bet that the agent isn't too enthusiastic about selling homes—or, at least, selling that home. Who has the most enthusiasm? Generally, the newer agent. We insiders say that the new agent doesn't know it can't be done, so he does it. In this chapter, we'll talk about the pros and cons of choosing a newer agent to work with.

What about level of knowledge? You want someone who knows a lot, don't you? Yes, but . . . it depends on how the agent drops that knowledge on you. Some agents try to impress you, overwhelming you with facts and figures—before they've even asked your name. These agents are so busy telling you everything they know, that they don't find out what you'd *like* to know. This is the kind of agent that causes buyers to complain that "the agent didn't listen." With information available today to you from many sources, you needn't be impressed by mere knowledge. Be impressed by an agent who listens to you, then gathers and prioritizes information in a thoughtful, meaningful way. Could that be a newer agent? I think so.

What about the last quality, honesty? Most buyers want to work with an agent who is honest, both with them and with other parties to the transaction. However, you can't determine whether a person is honest by asking directly, "Are you honest?" A person demonstrates his honesty through his actions. But, you don't want to start working with an agent and find out, through his actions, the agent isn't honest. Then, it's too late. How are you going to find an honest agent? By checking references. That's why the best source of candidates for your agent is referrals. They can tell you whether an agent has acted honestly.

Besides the qualities I've listed, what other qualities are you looking for in a real estate agent? Two of my favorites are tenacity and assertiveness. I want an agent who doesn't give up, because I may need him to go to bat for me during a difficult negotiation. I want him assertive enough that he won't back down if he's bullied by a listing agent or a seller. Take a minute and jot down the qualities you're looking for.

The Qualifying Questionnaire

In Chapter 2, I gave you five questions to ask an agent when you "bump into" one. However, to do a thorough qualifying interview, you really need to ask more questions than that. I've created a list of questions that will reveal the business practices, values, and skills of your prospective choice. I suggest you use the questionnaire in Figure 3.1 in the consultation, that one- to two-hour formal meeting with an agent, where you'll get real estate information, qualify your agent, and make your final choice of agent.

Besides helping you choose a good agent, using this questionnaire lets the agent know you're serious about your choice, and you're a buyer who expects a high level of service. Now, let's look at the questions. I'll point out what to look for in each answer.

FIGURE 3.1 • Choosing Your Real Estate Agent: A Questionnaire

1. Is this your full-time career?

2. What percent of your income is derived from residential real estate sales?

3. How much time, on average, do you spend a week on residential sales?

4. How many buyers do you work with at once?

5. How much time will you have for us?

6. What percent of your transactions come from listings? From sales?

7. What areas do you specialize in? What price ranges? What kinds of buyers?

8. Will you work with other buyers in the same price range while you're working with us?

9. What are your sales strengths? Have you taken courses in negotiation? How do you hone your sales skills?

10. Are you a member of the REALTOR® association?

11. Who would you represent in a transaction? Why?

12. How will you assist us with research, financing, negotiations, and follow-up before and after closing?

13. Tell us about your company and office. Do you have part-timers? Do you have minimum performance standards? Is it tough to get hired? Do you have ongoing education? What's important to your company and office?

14. How does your office/company handle complaints?

15. Do you expect loyalty, or do you work with anyone?

16. What criteria do you use to choose the buyers you work with?

17. Will you expect us to look at homes on our own? If so, why?

Agent has shown:

❏ Portfolio or brochure

❏ Five or more letters of recommendation

❏ Education/training credentials

❏ A statement of how the agent works

❏ Disclosure of agency form

1. Is this your full-time career? You obviously want someone who treats real estate sales as a career, not an avocation. I don't recommend you work with a part-timer. In my opinion, a part-timer is anyone who devotes less than 40 hours a week to selling real estate.

2. What percent of your income is derived from residential real estate sales? You are looking for someone who derives most of his income from residential sales, not commercial sales, property management, or some other source of real estate income. Why? You want an agent who specializes in selling residential properties.

3. How much time, on average, do you spend a week on residential sales? The average agent spends 50 hours a week at work. You want someone dedicated to the business, ready to work with you when you have time. You don't want to fit your schedule into a part-time agent's availability.

4. How many buyers do you work with at once? Be wary of the high-producing agent who may not have time for you. If the agent tells you he works with as many buyers as he can find, you'll know he's not choosing his buyers carefully. On average, good agents work with no more than six to eight buyers who will buy in the next one to three months from them.

5. How much time will you have for us? Although you want an agent who's available when you want to look at homes, you also want a successful agent. Finding the balance between the two is your job. A reasonable amount of time would be available to tour homes once to twice a week.

6. What percent of your transactions come from listings? From sales? The first question means the agent represents sellers, marketing their homes to other agents and to the public; the second means the agent is selling houses to buyers like you. You want someone who sells enough real estate in a year to be well practiced. In my opinion, anything less than eight sales to buyers (not listings sold) in a year isn't enough to qualify to be my agent. (Some agents' businesses are heavily slanted toward listing properties. They're not as interested in you as a buyer.)

7. What areas do you specialize in? What price ranges?

What kinds of buyers? Get a sense about whether this agent knows enough about your needs to really provide service. If she says she'll show you homes in the entire state, run the other way. You want an agent who has sold houses to other buyers like you, so that agent has identified with your needs, and is interested in helping buyers like you. Some agents, for example, won't work with first-time buyers, while other agents specialize in helping first-time buyers.

8. Will you work with other buyers in the same price range while you're working with us? Some agents who

represent buyers will not do this, because it puts their buyers in competition with each other. To avoid this situation, a good buyer's agent will refer you to another buyer's agent.

9. What are your sales strengths? Have you taken

courses in negotiation? How do you hone your sales skills? Listen to determine whether this agent is learning new communication and negotiation skills continually by taking courses such as the Dale Carnegie Sales Course. Or, whether he believes that one sales course taken five years ago prepared him for the competitive world of real estate sales today.

10. Are you a member of the REALTOR® association? About half of all real estate licensees nationally are

REALTORS®. That means they join the professional organization for real estate salespeople, the National Association of REALTORS®, and pay their $300 dues annually. REALTOR® members abide by the REALTOR® Code of Ethics, take more educational courses than other licensees, earn more money and generally exhibit a higher level of professionalism than licensees who are not REALTORS®. I recommend you work with a REALTOR®.

11. Who would you represent in a transaction?

Why? Is the agent going to represent you? If not, why not? Listen to see how the agent explains agency choices. In the next chapter, we'll explain your agency representation options.

12. How will you assist us with research, financing, negotiations, and follow-up before and after closing?

Listen as the agent explains how she works. Does it sound organized and well thought out? The agent should describe how she will search out homes for you, how she will tour with you, and how she will strategize with you prior to your making an offer on a property. If the plan doesn't sound well thought out, keep going to the next candidate.

13. Tell us about your company and office. Do you have part-timers?

Do you have minimum performance standards? Is it tough to get hired? Do you have ongoing education? What's important to your company and office? Your agent should be stating solid business practices, and, through his actions, should reflect the business values of his office. Also, you may have to work with another agent in the office, or the broker. Do you sense this would be an entirely different experience from working with this agent? In other words, you may be talking to the only competent agent in the office!

14. How does your office/company handle complaints?

One of the biggest surprises you could get is when you have a complaint with the agent or company. Now's the time to find out how complaints are handled. Ask the agent about procedure. Does the office and company have a process for handling buyer complaints? Ask the agent how that works. Many offices and companies have no planned, formalized process. So, if you have a complaint, you have a challenge even in getting someone's attention!

15. Do you expect loyalty, or do you work with anyone?

Does the agent take enough pride in his work that he refuses to work with buyers who do not commit to him? Good agents work only with buyers they trust. Loyalty is the foundation of that trust.

16. What criteria do you use to choose the buyers you work with?

How choosy is the agent? Good agents are careful about who they work with, for they're working for long-term referrals, not one sale. A competent agent works only with those they've qualified financially, and those they feel are motivated to purchase. In addition, they work with people with whom they want to have a long-term business relationship.

17. Will you expect us to look at homes on our own? If so, why? Good agents don't just give a buyer a list of homes to see, and then write the offer after the buyer has found the home of his choice. Instead, they stay with the buyer every step of the way, to ensure that he gets the information he needs and sees properties right for him. Only in a very fast market would a good agent give you a list of homes to see on your own. After all, you should be relying on the judgment and the comments of the agent as you both tour together, to give you information to make good property choices.

Other documentation.   In addition to asking the questions above, I recommend you gather other evidence of an agent's qualifications:

- Her brochure or portfolio—some evidence of who she is and how she works
- At least five letters of recommendation, or a list of people with whom the agent has worked whom you can call for references
- Education and training credentials, to show the agent keeps her education current
- A statement of how the agent works. The list of services in Figure 3.2 is an example of the type of list you may get from your agent. If your agent doesn't offer one, ask for such a list. Specifically, the services agents can provide depend on their agency relationship with you.

Four Considerations in Choosing a Competent Agent

Now, you're armed with a questionnaire and a list of documentation to obtain. Next, we'll look at four other considerations you'll have in choosing your agent:

1. New or experienced
2. Levels of production
3. Levels of education
4. Broker's license—or not

FIGURE 3.2 • List of Agent Services

My Personal Commitment to You

I WILL

Counsel with you to find out your particular need in a home, explain the purchasing process, and give you pertinent purchasing information.

Educate you about the financial market, new loan programs, and up-to-date market information, so we can establish your price range and loan preferences early and accurately.

Recommend professional, experienced mortgage brokers who will assist you in choosing a financial program best suited for your needs.

Preview all homes before showing, to ensure that our time together is productive.

Research and follow up on any homes, signs, or ads you may see; this saves you time and assures you that only homes matching your needs will be shown to you.

Consistently re-evaluate the purchasing process with you as we continue, so we're certain that we are on track

Communicate with you on a regular basis, return your phone calls, and gather information as requested.

Present and negotiate your purchase and sale agreement in a professional, skillful manner.

Follow up on your transaction during the processing stage; coordinate communication between you and the seller, loan company, escrow company, and listing agent; keep you informed of the progress of the transaction.

Enlist the support and knowledge of our manager to counsel with me on any considerations that may arise.

Be a reference source for you to help find school information, utilities, and special services.

If appropriate, *attend closing* with you.

Arrange possession of your new home and coordinate between you and the seller.

Check back with you regularly after closing to ensure that you are happily resituated in your new home; my main objective is a satisfied customer.

MY GOAL is to create a real estate relationship with you so strongly that you will refer me to your friends and business associates. I want to become your "real estate adviser for life"!

1. New or Experienced?

New agents.   Most of you would say you don't want a new agent. But, how "new" is too new? It isn't the amount of time the agent has been in the business. Whether the newer agent is competent to work with you depends on the following:

- The agent's prior life experiences (her job, her talents, her abilities)
- The training and mentoring she's gotten since she started in the real estate business
- The number of transactions she's completed since she entered the business.

Most new agents start with little help. The manager's motto is, "Here's your desk, here's your phone, you're on your own." This is especially true in the large offices. So, most new agents start slowly, and take months to close their first transactions. It takes them a year to get a little experience in sales. Of course, I don't recommend this kind of new agent.

However, not all newer agents start slow. I have hired and coached new agents, who, in their first year, became more capable than ten-year agents. What was the difference? I provided them a fast-track training and start-up program, along with a dynamite coach to help them implement my systems. The new agents themselves had the smarts and backgrounds that were natural segues into real estate. At the end of their first year, they had sold twice as many properties as most of the more experienced agents in my office.

What do fast starters have? Enthusiasm, lots of energy, and great desire to do a terrific job for you. They're not just after the money, either. They're after the referrals. They want you to be so pleased with their service that you'll refer them to others to help them build careers. This kind of newer agent is a good choice, especially for a first-time buyer. They have the get-up-and-go to match a first-time buyer's energy level, and they're patient and willing to explain the fine points of purchasing. So, don't rule out those with less than one year of experience in the business—if they fit my qualifying guidelines.

Experienced agents.   You may be thinking that the experienced agent is always your best choice. Not necessarily. Being on the inside of the industry for a long time, I know how far behind the times many experienced agents are today. Yes, they have a wealth of historical knowledge, but they aren't developing the new strategies and business practices today as demanded by either the industry or consumers. They aren't investing in or learning the new technology. Experience alone is no longer an adequate teacher. If you are drawn to an experienced agent, be sure that agent is "with it," and has an enthusiastic attitude about learning new "tricks." As long as the agent has completed enough transactions to be well practiced, other considerations are more important than many more years of real estate experience.

Insider Secret

☞ Experience may be a poor teacher in today's rapidly changing real estate world.

2. Levels of Production

Low producers with experience. Many agents have been in the business a long time, but have completed few transactions. This combination, low production and many years of experience, is the worst choice for a buyer. Having been around the lingo a long time, these low-producing agents can talk a good game. They just can't *play* a good game! (Usually, they just don't bother to get in the game at all. Hence, their low production.) Their information is outmoded, their get-up-and-go has gone, and they are not excited about helping you—or in learning to do business a better way. As the president of a real estate company told me once, "Most agents aren't in the business 20 years; they're in the business one year, 20 times."

What would be considered a low producer? In my opinion, anyone completing fewer than eight to ten transactions in a year, with no less than six of these being sales. Earlier, we said that the average REALTOR® makes about $26,000 a year. That's about ten transactions, using average income nationally per transaction. Of course, in some areas, earning $26,000 means the agent sold 15 homes. While, in others, the agent might have sold only 6 homes. The variables are area home prices and the agent's share of the commission dollars. Since the public thinks agents make twice what they do, the public also concludes the chances of their working with a fairly successful agent are good. Not so. The chances are much greater that they'll bump into a low-producing agent. In our area (greater Puget Sound, Washington), the average number of transactions completed each year per licensee (that's sales and listings sold) is *four.* That includes REALTORS® and those who are not REAL-TORS®—all the licensed folks selling real estate in our area. So, your chances of working with a low-producing agent in my city are great. All the more reason to use that questionnaire and qualify your agent carefully.

The top producer.   Many buyers think choosing the top agent in the office guarantees them the best service, but I'm not so sure the top agent is always the right choice. As manager of a real estate office, I'd often get a call from a prospective buyer, who wanted me to refer her to my top agent. When I got those calls, I would immediately ask the buyer what kind of agent she was looking for. Where did she want to look at homes? At what price range? I was trying to help the buyer develop criteria for choosing an agent that was important to that particular buyer. Most of the time, I didn't recommend that she work with the top agent in the office, but the best agent for her. This, of course, was an agent who met certain production standards, as well as meeting the buyer's qualifying criteria (such as working with first-time buyers).

Sometimes, the top agent is the very worst choice for a particular buyer. I know, from working experience, many first-time buyers are scared to death of getting coerced into purchasing a home. It takes a patient agent with a bent for educating to work well with first-time buyers. The top producer may not have time or patience for them. Many top agents are so busy they won't even work with first-time buyers.

Each individual buyer has his own needs, his own pace. There's a good agent to meet each of those needs, and it may not be the top agent in the office. What you should be concerned with is finding an agent with an infectious enthusiasm for working with you and learning new skills. That type of agent will go to the ends of the Earth for you, and will maintain your business relationship long after you've moved into your new home.

Top agents with assistants.   For the last few years, top agents have hired assistants to help them organize and run their businesses. When this phenomenon first began, assistants did the support paperwork, much like an office manager would in your office. As agents hired more assistants, they created specialized jobs for each assistant. One assistant handled the marketing, another the transaction follow-up. Now, some assistants even sell. (They must be licensed to do so, and some states and real estate companies restrict the kind of activities assistants can do.)

In the situations where assistants sell, the "lead" agent has little day-to-day interaction with buyers. He's really just the "marquee name." These marquee name agents manage a team of assistants who do the actual selling. In reality, these mega-agents have become owners of real estate offices. Their offices function a bit differently from the traditional real estate office, but the organization consists of a manager and salespeople, the same as in the traditional real estate office.

Insider Secret

☛ Seeing your agent's face on a billboard may be as close to that agent as you're going to get (if you choose the mega-dollar agent).

If you choose one of these mega-agents, be prepared to work not with the "name" agent, but with one or more of his assistants. That's why I said the closest you may get to that mega-dollar agent you were referred to is the billboard picture. You don't want to be shuffled off to an assistant, at least not totally. Karyn Sandbeck, one of my agent advisers, suggests in your consultation you ask the agent how his assistant(s) will be working with you. Also, you should meet the assistant during the initial consultation. You'll need to be sold on both the agent and the assistant, since you'll be working with both.

Insider Secret

☛ Wowed by that caption on the business card that states "million-dollar club"? A million-dollar producer may not be able to buy your lunch.

The million-dollar producer. You'll see real estate business cards with the tag "million-dollar producer" or "multimillion-dollar producer," denoting a high producer—you think. With rising home prices, this type of recognition for high producers has pretty much lost its meaning. For instance, in San Francisco, selling a million dollars worth of property could mean you sold one of your listings priced at $500,000—all year. Here's how agents figure out how many millions of dollars of properties sold the agent can brag about. It's generally accepted practice to count each side of the transaction (listing and selling sides) toward bragging rights. So, if I sold a $500,000 property I had listed, I would get to count that $500,000 twice—since I made two commissions from it (the list side, and the sale side). Boy, I had a great year. I sold one home!

If I were selling in Keokuk, Iowa, a million-dollar acknowledgment on my business card would mean something entirely different. I would be one of the higher-producing agents in the state of Iowa, in terms of numbers of homes sold, because the average home price in Keokuk is likely about $125,000. Because of its widely varying meaning, dollar volume or the million dollar club is not used nearly as much as it used to be to describe how agents are doing.

If you are qualifying an agent who has "million-dollar club" or "multimillion-dollar club" on his card, ask these questions: How many homes did you sell? How many of your listings sold? That's what you really want to know. How many times did he practice his skill? How many buyers did he make happy last year? You want an agent who has practiced his selling skills enough to lead you through this buying process with confidence.

Insider Secret

☞ When the initials *after* the name are longer than the agent's name, you may be getting someone whose principal occupation is student, not salesperson.

3. Levels of Education

Agents with accreditation. Some licensees seem to gather educational courses and designations to see if they can actually fill a business card. Right now, too, designations seem to be "the thing"—and some of them take little effort to earn. I don't even know what many of those initials stand for, and I've been involved in teaching designation courses for over a decade. I'm an instructor for the Managers' Council of the National Association of REALTORS®, and teach two of the managers' courses leading to the CRB (Certified Real Estate Broker) designation. Even though I'm a believer in ongoing education, I know information absorbed or courses completed have little impact on competency, unless the information is put to work in the real world. Personally, I have found the courses that I have taken as a REALTOR® to be extremely valuable. However, I also give myself some credit, because I took the ideas I heard in class and translated them to actions in my office.

When you see designations on an agent's business card, ask the agent what those designations mean and how he uses the information he got in his business. Ask the agent to explain the criteria to earn that designation, and why he earned it. You'll be able to determine whether your agent has "designitis," or has truly applied what he learned in those courses to better meet your needs.

Should the agent be a REALTOR®?
The NAR is, by far, the largest professional association for real estate agents and brokers. Dues (local, state, and national), are about $300 per year. Similar to other professional, volunteer organizations, the NAR provides services to its members, including continuing education. Its REALTOR® Code of Ethics sets standards of practice for its members, and provides a means for consumers and REALTORS® to seek disciplinary actions against REALTORS® who don't abide by the Code.

My observation is that almost all serious, committed real estate licensees are REALTORS®. Find out if the licensee you're qualifying is a REALTOR®; if she isn't, ask why not. Listen closely to the answer, and ask yourself whether, in your line of work, that answer would suffice about your own professional organizations. Having been active in local, state, and national REALTOR® organizations in education for over a decade, I know how much I've learned, and how valuable the professional relationships are that I've created. I can't imagine selling or managing in this turbulent climate without the assistance of a national network like the NAR.

4. Broker's License—or Not

Isn't a broker a better choice for you than a mere agent? From this book, you know how a licensee earns a broker's license. You know that owners, managers, and agents all can earn brokers' licenses. An agent who has a broker's license is an associate broker. Although a manager must earn a broker's license to manage, in most states an agent doesn't have to earn a broker's license to continue selling. (A few states require all salespeople to become brokers after a few years of obtaining a salesperson's license.) If a salesperson doesn't have to earn a broker's license, why does he go to the time and expense of doing so? The broker's license is the best recognized differentiator of all the designations.

The public believes someone with a broker's license to have more knowledge and expertise than one who is a mere agent. Is that true? Kind of. At least, an agent who earns the broker's license thought enough about differentiating himself to spend hundreds of dollars and thousands of hours becoming educated, and many hours preparing for and passing a broker's license exam. I respect agents who earn their broker's licenses for that reason. If it came down to choosing two agents with the same qualifications, but one had a broker's license, I'd choose the agent with the broker's license. Is the agent with the broker's license always the better choice? No.

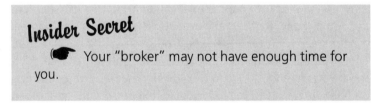

Insider Secret

☞ Your "broker" may not have enough time for you.

The real estate broker who manages an office and sells. Until ten years ago, most brokers who were managers had a full-time job managing the agents in their offices. Few managers also sold real estate, unless they were managing a very small office. This has changed dramatically in the past few years. In fact, a recent study by the NAR showed that 72 percent of those managing real estate offices today also sell. Why the trend? Shrinking company profits have forced managers to increase their incomes through selling and listing homes.

So, your chances of working with an agent who also manages an office (and has a broker's license, of course) are steadily increasing. If you are interviewing an agent with a broker's license, ask whether he also manages an office. How many agents does he manage? How much of his income is derived from managing, and how much from sales? How much time will he have for you? Although one can manage and sell, few managers do them both very well (just like any of us with two full-time jobs!).

Skills Your Agent Should Have

Besides the qualities, the sales history and skills revealed in the questionnaire, and the four critical areas listed in the previous section, I believe there are four skills your agent should have—in abundance:

1. Sales communication skills
2. Marketing skills
3. Negotiating skills
4. People skills

Having skill in these four areas ensure that your agent will be competent at what he does, and pleasant to work with.

1. Sales Communication Skills

My group of agent advisers stressed the need for you to find an agent with excellent sales communication skills. They underscored the need for listening skills, in particular. There are so many miscommunications that can occur during the buying process, that you need an agent who will listen carefully to your needs and ask good questions.

2. Marketing Skills

I think it's very important that agents have well-developed marketing skills. They will be promoting you to sellers when they bring your offer on your behalf. Ask to see the agent's brochure or portfolio to give you an idea of her background, organizational abilities, and ability to promote her strengths. You want to know she is confident enough to tell you the truth about something, even if you don't want to hear about it at the time (for instance, that this may not be the best home for you).

You want her to be confident enough to tell you when she thinks you're wrong. You don't want her so wishy-washy that she would tell you anything just to make you happy.

3. Negotiating Skills

I'll bet few buyers choose an agent because of the agent's negotiating skills. Yet, buyers are entrusting agents with hundreds of thousands of dollars of their money. As one agent says, her job is to "sell offers to sellers," not sell properties to buyers. I have seen the most atrocious negotiating skills at work in offer presentations—agents who literally cost buyers thousands and thousands of dollars. I have also seen agents who were masters at negotiating. Once you have signed that offer, you are almost never going to negotiate on your own behalf. Now it's all in your agent's hands. Be sure your agent has taken courses in negotiation. To find out how your agent views negotiation, ask him to sketch his method of preparing for and presenting offers on property. His description should be well thought out, with proven negotiating strategies, such as presenting the strongest points first.

4. People Skills

The last category is important, if broad. I've seen buyers' agents who ruined a buyer's chances at purchasing a property, just because they couldn't get along with the listing agent. Some agents go into offer presentations as though they're going to a fight. You can imagine what happens to that offer. Others go in ready to lose. Neither strategy is good for buyers. Some agents manage to make adversaries of all the parties when the transaction is being processed to close. I've seen buyers' agents get in screaming matches with buyers. Most of the time, these bad situations didn't have to occur. They were created and nurtured by agents with few people skills. As you're qualifying an agent, ask yourself if that agent will build bridges to the stressed-out personalities in the transaction, or will he tear them down? You want an agent who creates healthy business relationships. All in all, you want an agent who you'll enjoy spending time with.

The Ideal Agent

I've given you dozens of suggestions for choosing the right agent, from qualities to skills to questionnaires. As I wrote this chapter, I started thinking about the criteria *I* would use to choose an agent. So, turnabout is fair play—here's the kind of agent I'd look for if I were buying a home today:

- Has been in the business three to five years and seems really committed and enthusiastic
- Has completed higher level training (Graduate, REALTORS® Institute and Certified Residential Salesperson—both NAR-sponsored educational programs for real estate agents, which include sales and technical skills)
- Has completed an average of 10 to 20 sales per year or more (working with buyers)
- Has letters of recommendation, and a list of people I could contact
- Has a portfolio or brochure, with stated mission and values
- Specializes in the area where I want to look
- Has time to put me first, within reason
- Doesn't delegate me totally to an assistant
- Seems strong enough to tell me the truth, even if I don't like it
- Explanations about agency relationships and how he works are clear and concise
- Has high standards for choosing buyers
- Demonstrates strong communication skills
- Seems to match my business values

The Most Important Part of Your Buying Process

With a competent agent on your side, you can relax and actually have fun looking for and purchasing a home. In the next chapter, we'll explore the legal aspects of representation, and what various types of representation mean to you. Before you start the next chapter, though, list the qualities you want in an agent while they are fresh in your mind.

Frequently Asked Questions

Q. What should I do if I get halfway through the consultation, and discover I just don't *like* the agent nor do I want to work with her?

A. Explain to the agent that you don't think working with her is a "match." Thank her for her time and leave.

Q. I have a friend who was working with a real estate agent. Then, the agent quit calling, even though they had looked at several homes together. What's going on?

A. Maybe the agent left the business. Or, the agent may have decided that buyer wasn't serious about buying. Perhaps the agent got too busy to work with the buyer, or decided he just didn't like the buyer. Your friend should call the agent's manager and discuss the situation. The manager could help the buyer choose another agent.

Q. How many agents should I consult with?

A. I hope, only one. By the time you get to the consultation, you should have loosely qualified that agent, and should simply be finishing the qualifying process. However, if you haven't had a chance to qualify this agent at all, and find, after the consultation, you don't want to work with him, you'll have to find another agent and qualify him. You can do a shortened version of the consultation process with the second agent.

4

From Legalese to Real Life

What Kind of Business Relationship Do You Want with a Real Estate Agent?

The trend toward agents representing buyers as their clients is one of those seven important real estate trends I introduced in the first chapter of this book. In this chapter, I'll tell you how the trend is evolving and how it is changing the way buyers work with real estate agents. Now, buyers have choices of the type of representation they can get from agents. I'll explain what those choices mean to you, and what you should watch out for in each of the types of representation.

What is *buyer representation?* That means agents form a legal relationship with a buyer as a client, promising to fulfill several legal responsibilities. Along with these responsibilities come certain services, which, in sum, protect the client's best interests. Agents representing buyers form the same type of legal relationship agents form with sellers when they list properties for sale. Later in this chapter, I'll list what these legal responsibilities and services are to protect the client's best interests. First, here is a short history of how buyer representation has evolved.

The Transition to Representing Buyers

What Representation Means

Most of us have either listed a property with a real estate company or know someone who has. Since we have that frame of reference, let's look at that relationship to understand what it means to be represented. Let's say you are planning to sell your house. You'll probably enlist the services of a real estate company. You'll sign an "exclusive listing agreement," a contract in which you agree to pay a real estate commission to that particular company. In return, to earn its commission, the company agrees to provide certain services to market your property successfully. *Exclusive* means that this firm will be the only firm listing the property, and the only firm you'll pay when your home sells.

If you are listing your property like most sellers do, you'll be listing your property with a real estate company that is a member of the local multiple listing service (MLS). Through its agreement with the MLS, the company will pay part of the commission to the company that sells your property (usually split half-and-half between the company that lists the property for sale and the company that sells the property). Because you signed a contract with the company that listed your property, you are termed a "client," and you are legally represented by that company.

Once Upon a Time . . .

Most agents represented the seller. Sellers signed contracts for representation with their listing company. The client relationship formed when the seller signed the contract had far-reaching impact. All agents in that company, then, represented the seller, even if they were working with buyers. What if an agent in that company sold that house to a buyer? That agent was still working for the seller. That's not all. All other agents and other companies also represented the seller (unless they signed a contract with a buyer to represent a buyer). What about the agent in another company working with the buyer who bought the home? That agent also represented the seller, in a legal arrangement termed "subagency." So, who represented the buyer? No one unless the buyer expressly signed a representation contract with an agent. (Most buyers didn't realize they had no representation, though.)

Buyers were customers, not clients.   When a seller (or a buyer, if the laws allow) is legally represented by a real estate licensee, he's known as a client. As I said in the previous paragraph, the buyer, though, until a few years ago, generally had no legal representation. So, if the buyer had no legal representation, he couldn't be called a client. What was he known as? A customer. Does that mean he didn't get any services from an agent when he bought a home? No. Legally, agents can provide some services to those buyers who are their customers. You'll see, in Figure 4.1, the services and duties of an agent to a customer. These responsibilities are not more than one would expect of any businessperson. On the contrary, the buyer's agent's duties listed in Figure 4.2 are much more demanding of the real estate agent, requiring much more service to his "client."

All agents were to get the highest price for the seller.   The listing agent's job was to protect the best interests of the seller. That included getting him or her the highest price and best terms. But, because *all* agents represented the seller, even the agent who sold the house to a buyer had a legal duty to protect the seller's best interests—just like the listing agent.

Agents working with buyers as customers put agents in a quandary.   In reality, representing the seller's best interests was difficult for agents working with buyers. Why? Because the agents knew the buyers so much better than they knew the sellers.

Let me show you what I mean. I was referred to Joe and Sally Smith, buyers, by Joe's coworker, George Rally. I had sold a home to George, and he graciously told Joe I was the best agent he'd ever worked with. He assured Joe I would look out for their best interests, and get him a really great property—at a great price. You're already seeing some conflict, right? By the time I met Joe and Sally, they were already sold on me. And, of course, since agents build careers on referrals, I wanted Joe and Sally to think the same thing of me that George thought. As I showed Joe and Sally homes, I got to know all about them and their family. We became good friends, especially since Joe and Sally had been transferred to Seattle and had to buy a home quickly. We spent dozens of hours looking at properties, and Joe and Sally were expectedly stressed out. My job was to make the experience relatively painless—and to do such a great job they would refer more buyers to me. Finally, we found the home they wanted to purchase. The buyers,

---

FIGURE 4.1 • An Agent's Responsibilities to a Customer

Honesty—must disclose material facts; no fraud or misrepresentation

Fairness—make timely agency disclosures so that the customer can protect his interests; explain the differences between customer and client

Accounting—honor license laws requiring care of the moneys of others

Reasonable care and diligence—obey the laws and regulations pertaining to transactions

admittedly, expected me to help them create and present an offer that would be most favorable to them. And, as is usual, I had never met the seller. Yet, legally, I was expected to watch out for the seller's best interests—he was my "client." You can easily see the conflict real estate agents have faced as they worked with customers under traditional agency law.

Why Buyer Representation?

As you can imagine, the conflicts and confusion caused when all agents represented the seller resulted in, at worst, messy lawsuits. At the least, the laws and the practices of real estate agents caused frustration and disappointment from buyers and sellers. Part of the move toward licensees representing buyers, then, came as a result of the confusion caused by almost all agents representing sellers.

Real estate companies looked for other means of income. There were other pressures besides legal considerations to change buyers' relationships with licensees. As real estate profits dipped, companies and agents looked for other sources of revenue. They noted the industry had focused its efforts on sellers, with sellers' marketing tools, sellers' presentations, and sellers' advertising. As costs of representing sellers escalated, real estate companies looked to buyers for those needed sources of revenue. They noted, though, there were few services for buyers. So, slowly at first, real estate agents and a few real estate companies started representing buyers, developing specialized services as they refined their representation. This type of representation has caught hold, although some agents and agencies have been very resistant to these changes. A recent survey by the NAR showed that buyers had representation in 41 percent of the transactions.

FIGURE 4.2 • The Buyer's Agent: Fiduciary Duties to His Client

1. Undivided—loyalty act solely in the best interests of the client (buyer)
2. Obedience—act subject to the principal's (client-buyer) continuous control; do not exceed the scope of authority conferred by the principal; obtain and follow all lawful instructions
3. Reasonable care and diligence—protect the principal from foreseeable risks of harm; recommend that the principal obtain expert advice when the principal's needs are outside the scope of the agent's expertise
4. Confidentiality—refrain from communicating key personal information about the principal that was given or acquired by the agent within the scope of employment as an agent to the principal; personal information must be kept confidential unless the client releases the agent from this duty
5. Full disclosure—disclose affirmatively all information concerning the transaction that might affect the principal's best interests
6. Accounting—promptly report to the principal all money and property received and paid out; safeguard any money or property held on behalf of the principal

---

And, that number is growing. Three-quarters of the companies surveyed said they have agents who work as buyers' agents. Some agents now even specialize in representing buyers, and do not work with sellers, listing properties.

Laws changed to support buyer representation.

The practice of buyer agency, or buyer representation, has resulted in many states making laws about agency representation. For instance, in the state of Washington, all agents now represent the buyer, except the listing agent, who represents the seller. That law gives client-level representation to all buyers (see Figure 4.2).

In many states, though, the buyer is not automatically considered a client. Because laws differ from state to state, you must ask your agent to explain your agency choices.

To keep up with practice and law changes, the education of licensees has escalated. In 1996, the NAR bought the rights to the Real Estate Buyer's Agency Council, Inc. (REBAC). For the past few years, REBAC has offered a two-day course leading to the Accredited Buyer Representative designation (ABBR.). Now, about 1,000 agents are completing this course each month, resulting in thousands of agents holding the ABBR. designation. If you're looking for a buyer's representative, you may want to choose an agent with ABBR on his card. By the way, you can get a referral of a buyer's agent in another city by using the REBAC members' directory.

Realizing the need to educate managers about the management of buyer agents, REBAC has created a one-day course for owner-brokers, which is being offered nationally. I was a part of the team that developed the course. I've included the information here about designations and education to stress to you that agents and agencies are choosing to represent buyers, and learning what that representation means—whether or not their state laws require them to do so. Overall, I think buyer representation is a positive trend. Remember, though, you may be buying in a state where relatively few agents practice buyer representation. So, if you want buyer representation, you should ask for it.

The Nuts and Bolts of Buyer Representation

Legal responsibilities.   Following are the six legal responsibilities of buyers' representatives:

This is the type of representation you receive (from a legal definition) when you are a "client." It's the same level of service sellers have always received as clients of their agents. As you look at the list, you can see how the agent has agreed to protect your best interests. This type of representation results in a higher level of service than you will receive as a customer (that's because, if you're the agent's customer, the agent has a legal responsibility to the seller, his client, not you). So, if you're an agent's customer, the agent showing you homes will be representing the seller; thus, the agent must look out for the seller's best interests, not yours. If the agent inadvertently provides you a service that hurts the seller's best interests, he has violated his responsibilities to the seller.

Services for customers, services for clients.   Let me give you an example of how certain agent services can differ, depending on whether the buyer is a customer or a client of the agent. An agent working with a buyer as a customer shouldn't provide a market analysis on the home the buyer wants to buy. Why? Because the market analysis might show the seller's price is too high. Since the seller is the agent's client, the market analysis can't be done, for it would hurt the seller's negotiating position, and would not be protecting his best interests. However, if the agent is representing the buyer, she has a responsibility to provide a market analysis to the buyer, because, in that case, the buyer's best interests must be protected. And, a market analysis is in the client's (buyer's) best interests. With the assistance of his agent, the buyer will be able to use the market analysis to prepare an offer.

Services buyers can expect as clients. If you're a buyer, and you're an agent's client, you have the benefit of many services that are in your best interests. Here are a few of them. Your agent should do the following:

- Tell you how long a property has been on the market.
- Show you a "for sale by owner" property.
- Tell you if she thinks the seller may take less than list price for the property.
- Act under your (buyer's) instructions.
- Help you create a negotiating strategy.
- Provide a comparative market analysis, or counsel you on price.
- Disclose that the seller made a counteroffer to another buyer last week at a certain price.
- Call property owners in a particular area to see if any of the owners want to sell.
- Show you homes above the price you said you want to see—or can afford.
- Notify you about new properties on the market before notifying buyers who are customers.
- Use negotiating techniques on your behalf to get the seller to accept your offer.
- Tell you that a property is overpriced.
- Find the best property for you.
- Suggest a minimum deposit.
- Suggest that your offer be contingent upon your agent presenting the offer to the seller.
- Obtain a commission agreement with a "for sale by owner" property to pay the buyer's agent's fee on your behalf. (The owner is selling the home himself without a real estate agent representing him.)

- Suggest that you view the property at various times to see traffic patterns, etc.
- Call your attention to any negatives of a floor plan.
- Continue to show properties to you during the time you are negotiating to buy a particular property.
- Place "property wanted" ads to find an appropriate property for you.
- Tell you that the seller's agent indicated that the seller will accept less than list price.

In your best interests as a buyer, these are all services that can help you find the property of your choice and save you thousands of dollars. That's why I recommend you work with a competent buyer's agent.

An evolving profession.   The laws and practices regarding representing buyers vary greatly among states. The interpretation of these laws, and the practices, too, vary greatly among companies and real estate agents. The result is that buyers are receiving all levels of service. Marcie Roggow, an expert on buyer representation and one of the creators of an excellent video on buyer representation (listed in the "Other Helpful Sources" section), tells me that in some states, agents switch back and forth at will with the kind of representation they're providing—to the same buyer! This puts the agent in a precarious position legally, and will really confuse a buyer. It will take a few years until buyer representation gets more standardized, and agents learn how to deal with it.

Making an informed choice.   You must be informed about the agency law in your state early on in your conversations with an agent. You have your choice as to the kind of representation you want. This disclosure should be "timely"—that is, prior to the time a licensee enters into "substantive discussions" with the buyer or seller regarding real estate needs and financial capabilities (that's probably before the consultation). In a few states, agency disclosure can be verbal. In many states, it must be in writing. Marcie Roggow says that, although disclosure is the law, sometimes agents just don't get around to it. Some are uncomfortable explaining agency relationships; some just "forget."

To make sure you know your representation choices, Marcie recommends that you tell the agent you want the explanation in writing.

Companies, REALTOR® associations, and state licensing departments have created brochures explaining your representation options in the state where you're buying. All agents should have a brochure available to buyers.

A good resource. Having seen several videos on agency, I think the educational vehicle for you is Creative Learning Concepts' video, *Agency Relationships in Buying or Selling a Home*. Many agents have this video, so you can check with your agent to see if it's available through him. (If you want to order it yourself, see the "Other Helpful Sources" section.)

Keep your comments to yourself. Because agents represent one side or the other of a real estate transaction, and have a responsibility to protect their clients' best interests, you must be careful what you say to any agent besides your own buyer's representative. By law, agents are required to pass along to their clients any information they know could help that client. (Your buyer's agent, on the other hand, has promised not to disclose information you have told him that could be hurtful to you.) Be careful as you chat with agents as you make ad calls or as you visit open houses. You don't know who that agent represents until he discloses it. For example, my agent advisers stressed that you shouldn't disclose anything to a listing agent that you wouldn't want passed on to a seller. If you visit open houses and talk to the listing agent, don't tell the listing agent that you must buy in three days! The listing agent represents the seller and will tell the seller exactly what you said. You don't want the seller to know you have to move, because you will have reduced your negotiating power if you decide to make an offer on that property.

Going overboard. We all love to hate attorneys, because of their "win at all costs" reputation. Attorneys build their reputations, and big bucks, by winning big and causing big loss to the other party. (In defense of many great attorneys, my sister among them, the best do not ascribe to this modus operandi.) The single representation arrangement that attorneys have always worked under encourages that kind of outcome. You'd better hire an attorney to put you on the winning side, while putting the other guy in the loss column.

With the advent of single-client representation in real estate, I see that same danger. Some buyer representatives have become overzealous in their support of buyer representation. To prove their point, they seem to go overboard to represent the best interests of buyers. In this book, I'll give you several examples of situations where an agent has advocated so well on behalf of his client, he's cost the client a transaction, or at least, ruined a relationship and caused a lawsuit. Buying a home should be a win for everyone involved. After all, you don't want the seller to think he's lost to you, do you? That seller has a lot of power over that property until you get the key. You want the seller thinking the best of you, and cooperating in every way.

Working with a Buyer's Agent

You've decided to find a buyer's agent, for you like the level of service buyers' agents can provide. In this section, I'll discuss several aspects of working with a buyer's agent, including contracts and commissions.

Agents have represented sellers as clients for years. A seller contracted with a real estate company to sell his home. The seller signed an employment contract, called an exclusive listing agreement, and agreed to pay a commission to that company for services rendered. Now, buyers' representatives are asking buyers to sign the same kind of employment contracts, which spell out the client relationship, the services the buyer's representative will provide, the fees for services rendered, and the contract time frame. In this section, I'll discuss several of the points you'll want to consider in these agreements. Laws differ in every state, so I'll attempt to give you major considerations to look for. Armed with this information, you can decide if you want to sign such an agreement, and any stipulations you want to provide for in the agreement.

A Contract or Not?

Can you work with a buyer's agent without signing a contract? Yes, but because of the confusing nature of current agency law now, I recommend you do sign a buyer agency agreement when you're sure of the agent you want to work with. Putting your agreement on paper makes sense. You have asked the agent for a very high level of commitment— the same kind of commitment you ask of a listing agent when selling your property. After all, you're paying a healthy commission (which we'll discuss later in this chapter). You may also get the quality of service and reputation that should come along with that commission. Buyer's representation contracts is a growing trend. Of the buyers who used a buyer's agent in 1996, 87 percent had a written agreement.

Why Limit Yourself to One Agent?

You should limit yourself to one agent for the same reason sellers limit themselves to one listing agent—better service. When the agent knows there's a commission somewhere down the line, she'll be more committed to the buyer or seller. Even before buyers' agency, I discovered that working with buyers who worked with every agent and his brother just wasn't any fun (well, at least it seemed like those buyers worked with every agent in the area). I wanted to provide great service to the buyers. To do that, I had to spend lots of time discovering their needs, educating them about the market, the trends, the areas, financing, etc. Most of all, I wanted to establish a long-term relationship of trust and confidence. That seemed impossible when buyers worked with several real estate agents. Instead of focusing on getting buyers the right home, I found myself racing to properties faster than the other agents could find them. My commitment level was low, because I knew the buyers weren't committed to me. After enduring several of these situations, I quit working with buyers who refused to be loyal.

What does this mean to you? If you choose a buyer's agent with the guidelines I've suggested, you will get the highest level of service. You won't feel you must tell ten agents the kind of home you want, because you're afraid you'll miss something. Remember, all agents have the same information sources. A competent agent does much more than find homes for you. Those services require dedication, persistence, and putting you, the client, first. Being loyal, in return, is a small price to pay for this dedication.

Real Life

Pam and Bob Gains were referred to me from a firm in Ohio. They arrived in Seattle anxious to find a home for their family. As I showed them homes, I felt Pam didn't quite trust me. We'd be driving along, and she'd ask me the same question she asked me three days ago. I discovered that Pam and Bob had been looking for homes with another agent, too. Then, those questions made sense. Pam was testing me against the integrity of the other agent! That realization took away my trust in them. I really wondered why I should work so hard for them, keeping their needs in mind, when they were creating a "run-off" between me and the other agent. I knew unless I found the home they wanted first, the other agent had won. I started wondering how I could show them more homes faster—and how I could convince them to buy one of those homes, instead of buying from the other agent. However, I just couldn't become the "hard closer."

Finally, I sat down with them and asked them to choose one agent. As Karyn Sandbeck, a buyer's representative specialist, says, "Some agents think it is their job to close buyers on properties." That certainly becomes the case if buyers pit one agent against another. Not having loyalty also could discourage me from telling Pam and Bob some hard facts, even though they might need the information, for they could go to the other agent. In the end, Pam and Bob chose to work with me, and we found the perfect home for them—and created a trusting, long-term business relationship.

The Buyer Agency Agreement

The use of a buyer's agency agreement or contract varies widely from state to state and from agent to agent. Some agents never even tell the buyer that he can have a written agreement with the agent for services and representation. If a contract ensures buyer loyalty, why wouldn't agents use buyer agency agreements? There are several reasons. One favorite agents give is they don't need a buyer's agency agreement to spell out how special their services are. These agents say, "I'll prove I'm worth their loyalty by the way I work." Well, there's a problem with that. You, the buyer, don't have any frame of reference. That agent may be working really hard for you. But, unless you just had an experience where you felt another agent really dropped *your* ball, you really don't know what "hard work" is. You probably don't even know you're *supposed* to be loyal! Another reason agents don't use buyer agency agreements is they just don't think they're worth it. Or, they don't have the confidence to ask you to sign an agreement.

You should look for a buyer's agent who thinks he's worth the commission he charges; he expects loyalty because he knows he's *good*. Agents who use contracts, in my experience, have high service expectations of themselves, and aren't afraid they can't meet them. This type of agent is confident enough in his own abilities that he will negotiate strongly in your behalf. You don't want him wilting in front of a strong seller or listing agent!

The whole issue of buyer agency contracts—and buyer agency practice—varies dramatically from state to state. Here, I'll discuss a few points that you may see in a buyer agency contract. If you don't see these points, ask the agent how these considerations would be handled.

How Long Should the Contract Be in Effect?

As I mentioned earlier, buyers look at eighteen homes on average before making a buying decision. How long will it take you to find a home? Your contract should extend for a reasonable amount of time, long enough for you to find a home. Signing an agreement with a very long term is discouraging, I think, to both buyer and agent. Conversely, signing a very short agreement is just unrealistic. Talk to the agent about time considerations.

Canceling Your Contract

Can you get out of an agreement if you find you don't want to work with the agent? Yes. Your contract will spell out the terms. Find out how to terminate an agreement before the end date. Generally, these agreements require you to give termination notice to the broker or agent *in writing.* Be aware that, if you buy a home from another agent during the period within which you had promised to purchase a home from the agent with whom you signed the agreement, the first agent may attempt to collect the commission. Knowing how to terminate an agreement before you sign an offer with another agent will save you some unpleasant situations, at the least.

Who Pays the Commissions?

In most instances, the seller will pay the full commission. Why? Most properties you will look at are listed in the local multiple listing service. Through his exclusive listing agreement marketed by the local MLS, the seller agrees that the listing agency will pay part of the total commission to the company that brings a buyer. In some situations, however, the buyer pays part or all of the commission. Your buyer agency agreement should spell out who pays the fees and the amount of the fees for various situations. These include the following:

- Fees on properties listed with an MLS
- Fees on properties not listed with an MLS (like "for sale by owner" properties)
- Fees on presale/custom homes when the builder is introduced to the buyer by the agent
- Fees on lease/lease option/rental properties
- Fees on exercising an option

Payment by the buyer for commissions due is getting more and more common. In 1996, 20 percent of the buyers who had written contracts with buyers' agents, compensated the agent directly. You'll see this as a continuing upward trend.

When are the fees due?   Commissions are due when you close on a transaction, default on a transaction, or terminate the agreement to avoid paying a fee. In addition, if you purchase a home that the buyer's agent introduced to you during the term of your agreement, fees are due if this event occurred within a certain number of days of termination of the agreement.

Let's look at that last situation. If your buyer agency agreement says that you must purchase the home from the agent who showed you the property (within a time frame, of, generally, 120 days), you'd better be sure you do just that. If you sign an agreement, look at homes, and then find you do not want to purchase one of those homes from that agent, be sure you terminate your agreement with that agent in writing prior to signing an agreement with another agent. Be sure, too, if you purchase a home with your new agent, a home you saw with the first agent, you are not going to get into a dispute over who gets the commission. When in doubt, check with an attorney.

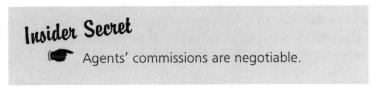

Insider Secret

☞ Agents' commissions are negotiable.

Pay less and get the same service?   Just as sellers can negotiate commissions when signing a listing agreement, so can buyers. Whether it's a smart thing to do, though, is questionable. What you're after is a high level of service. When you negotiate down your commission with your buyer's agent, you're probably assuming you'll get the same level of service. How do you guarantee the service level will stay the same as if you had paid more for it? That's a hard question to answer. Buyers have no such problem when they negotiate the price down on products. If it's the same product, it doesn't change, even though you pay less for it. For example, if you pay $40,000 or $30,000 for the same Cadillac, you're still getting the same product for your money.

If you're like most buyers, you never want your agent to put you second. Negotiating a lower commission sets the stage for demotivating an agent from putting you first. You've also asked the agent to be unfair to his other clients who are paying more for the same level of service. If your agent represents five purchasers, your agent has agreed to provide them all top-quality service—just like you want. The other four purchasers have agreed to pay your agent a commission of x percent. You, though, decide that, as a smart businessperson, you'll negotiate down that commission. So, you tell that agent that, although you want top quality service, and you expect that agent to put you first, you want to pay less for top-quality service. You can predict what will happen when the agent has to decide who to work hardest for.

What we are paid speaks directly to us in how we feel you value us. You feel the same way in your business. Let's say George and you hold exactly the same position. You find out George got a raise. You go to your boss and ask for the same raise. Your boss tells you that you're not getting a raise, but you are just as fantastic an employee. How do you feel? Devalued. What changes about how you view your boss and the company? Do you feel as loyal to the company as you did before? Are you motivated to work hard and support the company programs? The same thing happens to a competent agent when you try to negotiate commissions down at the beginning of the agreement. The agent becomes subconsciously demotivated.

Some agents will work for less.   You can always find agents who are willing to work for smaller commissions. They don't think they're worth larger commissions. My observation is—they're not. Another insider observation is, if you don't pick your agent well, no matter how low a commission you are able to negotiate, you won't experience even mediocre service.

The best solution is to work with a competent agent who charges a fair commission. When you find a competent agent, you will be paying much less for the service than the value you get. A good agent, dedicated to protecting your best interests, can save you thousands of dollars at the negotiating table, much more than you'll save by negotiating commissions with a less competent agent.

Retainers.   This is a fee that agents charge to enter into a buyer agency agreement. Karyn Sandbeck, an exclusive buyer's representative, charges a nonrefundable retainer fee, and she limits the number of buyers she works with. Although it's unusual now to charge a retainer, I think that this will be a growing trend. Why? Because buyers' agent specialists list no properties. They restrict their income sources to sales. Working with buyers is very time-consuming, so these agents must use that time in the most productive means possible. They are beginning to realize that the long and challenging process of being a buyer's agent is worthy of charging some money upfront. In most cases, the retainer fee is credited toward any fee owed to the broker. On termination or default of the contract, the retainer fee is retained by the broker. Find out how common retainer fees are in your area.

Dual Agency

So far, we've discussed two choices you have for representation: client and customer. At the beginning of your relationship with your agent, you will choose the kind of representation you want, generally from the two choices (although other less popular choices are available in certain states, such as "facilitator" and "transaction broker."). When your agent is representing you as a client, you and he have formed a "single agency" relationship. That is, the agent has promised to represent only you. Remember, too, that an agent can represent only one party in a transaction as either a seller's or a buyer's agent. This arrangement works just fine unless you want to purchase a home from the agent who has listed it. To complicate matters even more, the listing agent could be someone you just met at a public open house, or, it could be your buyer's agent! In these cases, the agent cannot represent you, because he already is representing the seller. So, he must either refer you to some other agent who will act as your buyer's agent, or become a "dual agent," representing both of you.

How Dual Agency Is Created

Let's say you walk into an open house, meet the listing agent (who represents the seller), and decide you want to purchase the house. First, the listing agent must disclose he is representing the seller. You know that he can't represent you, because he's already "spoken for." But, you want to buy the home from that listing agent.To work with you, he must ask you for permission to act as a "dual agent," that is, he would become an agent for both you and the seller. But, that's not all. In acting as agent for both parties, the agent also must reduce the level of representation he can provide either party. The dual agent cannot provide undivided loyalty to opposing clients. In addition, his duty of confidentiality to one client is naturally in conflict with the duty of full disclosure to the other client.

Your Agency Disclosure Addresses Dual Agency

The agency disclosure statement made up by the real estate company that you saw, and perhaps signed early in your relationship with the agent, will ask the buyer and seller to help the brokerage company resolve the conflict of representation. The statement will allow the brokerage company to modify its legal duties. The result, from your perspective, is that you get a drastically reduced level of representation. Although buyers purchase homes from listing agents often, they don't realize the legal ramifications. In this chapter and later chapters, I've given you some insider secrets to help you decide whether you want to buy a home from a listing agent.

Knowing When You're Getting into Dual Agency

How do you know when you're entering into a dual agency situation? Legally, when you are about to enter into any kind of a dual agency relationship (and there are many situations where this could happen), the agent must disclose all the facts and consequences, including the real effect on your interests. When agents don't disclose an impending dual agency relationship, they create what is called "undisclosed dual agency," and it's always illegal. Why? Because you haven't been made aware that the type of representation you agreed to has changed.

Insider Secret

☛ Being a dual agent can be as difficult as being engaged to two people—it isn't in your best interests.

Should You Accept Dual Agency?

No matter what a listing agent says to you to make you comfortable with dual agency, in practice, representing two people equally is very difficult. It would be like being engaged to two people (actually, my best friend was, and I marveled at how she arranged it—for a while!).Common sense tells us that the loyalties of the listing agent are naturally strongest with the seller. There are other problems with your accepting dual agency. When you enter into a dual agency relationship, the agent must not disclose confidential information given to him by a principal to another principal. That means, for example, that you can't get information from the agent you may need to design a successful negotiation. Why? Because what the dual agent knows about the seller's motivation to sell could hurt the seller's position. (Reread the duties listed in "The Buyer's Agent: Fiduciary Duties to His Client," earlier in this chapter.) Realize that you can have none of these services from your dual agent, because these services would jeopardize the position of the seller.

In most instances, you're better off not in a dual agency situation. This is especially true if you're thinking of purchasing a home from a listing agent you've just met in an open house. That's the most dangerous of all these agency situations, because you have no idea whether that agent is qualified to work with you, or where that agent's loyalties lie (more about this in Chapter 7). My advice is to avoid buying a home from a listing agent—go find a buyer's agent to represent you. Or, if you have an agent and want to buy a home he has listed, have him refer you to another agent who will represent you.

The Facilitator

There's one more type of relationship agents form with buyers. Some states allow real estate brokerages to act in a nonfiduciary capacity (not an agency capacity) for both parties in a transaction. This relationship is called "facilitator" or "transaction broker." The responsibilities are to exercise reasonable care and provide an accounting to all parties. Some states have additional legal duties, but in general, the facilitator role provides little service. I don't advise you to accept a facilitator when you can have a buyer's agent representing your best interests. The laws on agency representation vary from state to state; not all states offer all these choices of representation. Ask what the agent's responsibilities would be for any type of representation you are offered.

The Last Word on Buyer Representation

Buyer representation is a complicated, always changing issue. Get the straight scoop about agency law in your state from an agent who does a good job at explaining how the law works and what your options are. Remember too, get your options in writing.

Now, you're ready to get all the information on home buying in your consultation, and make a final choice on a real estate agent.

Frequently Asked Questions

Q. My friend bought a home from a listing agent and she had no problems. Why are you so wary of buying a home from a listing agent?

A. Because I've seen all the manipulative sales games listing agents play to get buyers to make offers on their properties. I know these listing agents are not concerned with the buyers' best interests; they're not even acting as a dual agent. They're just practicing "self-agency."

Q. I bought a home five years ago and I wasn't the client of my agent; I was the customer. Everything went fine. Why should I look for a buyer's agent?

A. It's true. Good agents are good agents. However, according to the law, agents are only supposed to provide the services listed earlier in this chapter when buyers are clients. Since about 50 percent of the buyers who bought homes in the last two years used buyers' representatives, I think you should try it. I think you'll be pleased with the level of service you find.

5

The Consultation

You're almost ready to start searching for homes in earnest. Almost. First, you'll want to sit down with an agent in the consultation, that one- to two-hour session where you both exchange information about home-buying and qualify each other. In this chapter, I'll show you what to expect during the consultation, and what you'll want to accomplish during the session.

What Do You Want from a Consultation?

During the consultation session, you'll want to accomplish the fol-lowing:

- Get information about the buying process.
- Describe the property you're looking for; find out what you can buy.
- Agree on the process you and the agent will use in finding you a home.
- Gather mortgage information and get qualifying guidelines.
- Make a final choice of agent.

You'll notice I said to "make a final choice of agent." You may have already chosen an agent prior to this consultation session. If so, I hope you used the five quick qualifying questions from Chapter 2. Many times, though, you will not have made the choice of agent prior to meeting the agent in this consulting session. If you're like most buyers, you still haven't, to this point, had much time to sit down and discuss the buying process in depth with an agent. Here's your chance to do that, and ask the questions of the agent posed in Chapter 3. You are looking for several skills and qualities in a real estate agent, and having this formal consultation allows you to qualify this agent to make a good choice.

Your Agent's Objectives

Your agent, too, has several objectives for this session. She wants to accomplish the following:

- Give you information about the buying process, including financing.
- Find out your buying needs, including property requirements.
- Explain agency choices and buyer representation contracts.
- Qualify you as a good prospect.
- Agree on the process you'll go about in finding a home together.

Taking the time to get to know each other, to gather the information you need, and to decide whether you want to work together makes the actual house-hunting much more pleasant.

Insider Secret

☞ Agents who are too eager to show you properties without getting to know your needs would be better suited to be tour guides at Disneyland.

The Nuts and Bolts of the Consultation

Who Makes the Appointment for the Consultation?

Either the buyer or the agent can start the consultation process. All agents, in my opinion, should arrange consulting sessions before putting buyers in their cars. But, some agents don't. So, if an agent you think you'd like to work with has not asked you to attend a consulting session, you can either ask the agent to provide one to you, or choose another agent.

Preparing for the Consultation

Before you attend the consultation, sit down with your buying partner, if you have one, and make a list of what you want in a property. Describe the setting, the area, and the amenities you want in the home. Decide what kind of down payment you want to invest. Gather a couple of pens and a notepad to take notes. Take the questionnaire from this chapter with you, too. By the way, you might expect agents to have the forms I've provided in this chapter. But, if they don't, bring the forms, just in case you need them.

Where Should the Consultation Take Place?

You may meet with the agent at the agent's office or at your home. I recommend going to the real estate office, because you'll be able to observe the office. Here are some things you'll want to evaluate:

- Businesslike atmosphere of the office: Are agents lounging in the entry, reading the newspaper, or generally acting as if they're vultures, waiting to pick off unsuspecting strangers? Or, are agents at their workstations, at work—just like you would be in your office?
- How businesslike is the business? Is the office clean, well organized, and ready for you as a buyer?
- Do you see evidence of business organization, like a vision or mission statement, information about the office style or operations?
- Is the support staff trained and capable in welcoming you?
- Is the broker/manager there? If so, attempt to meet the broker.
- Is the office equipped to meet your needs? Ask for an office tour.
- Look at the information sources. Check out the computers, resource room, and agents' workstations.

I am not asking you to judge the capabilities of the office and agent by whether the office is large or not. (We've discussed the shrinking office phenomenon—and the dangers of the mega-office.) Taking time to observe the office, its capabilities, and the people who work there, however, will give you a sense of how serious this office is in serving your needs. You're not just choosing the agent, you're choosing the office, too.

When Should You Arrange a Consultation?

Obviously, you want to get together with your prospective agent before you look at homes. How long before? It may be a few days; it may be a few months. It depends on your needs. Let's say you know you're getting a sales bonus in six months, and you'll be using that bonus as your down payment. It will take you anywhere from one week to eighteen weeks to locate a property, then a few days to negotiate, then six weeks to two months to close (on average). You will want to have your consultation three to six months before you get your sales bonus (if you want to buy when you get your bonus).

Discuss your situation with your prospective agent, and determine an appropriate time for this initial consultation A common mistake buyers make is to wait too long to get together with an agent. Good agents don't want to meet with you only when you have cash in hand and are ready to buy. Think of your competent agent as a real estate adviser, who wants to help you plan ahead, regardless of whether there's a commission for that agent in the next two months.

Insider Secret

☞ You may not qualify (and I don't mean financially) to work with the agent of your choice.

Will an Agent Always Agree to Meet with a Buyer?

No. Some agents act as though they are so desperate they would deal with any buyer anytime. But, good agents are careful about who they choose to work with. If an agent meets a buyer at an open house, for instance, and feels that it's not a good match, the agent will not make a further appointment. Or, after the agent meets with a buyer in a consultation session, and feels there's a personality conflict, the agent won't work any longer with the buyer. The following are some other reasons agents choose not to work with certain buyers:

- Buyers won't tell them the whole story about their buying situation.
- Buyers fib to them.
- Buyers are disrespectful, showing up late for appointments or missing appointments altogether.
- Buyers won't answer questions in the consulting session.

Good agents have guidelines they follow to accept or reject buyers. For a checklist that some agents use to make those decisions, see Figure 5.1.

Why don't agents just work with anyone—and everyone? It's impossible for agents to provide excellent service if they're working with too many buyers. Generally, an agent won't work with more than six or eight buyers at a time, especially if all these buyers will be buying in the next month or so. Also, a good agent chooses his buyers carefully, because he must have trust and confidence in them, as they have in him. Remember, a good agent is after referral business.

What You Can Expect in the Consultation

Although each agent has a different way of going about the consultation, I'll give you a general sense of the process. First, the agent finds out what you're looking for in a home. She'll provide you with information about what's available in the area. She'll tell you whether what you're looking for actually exists in your price range. She may educate you about the trends for the area, information you'll put to use as you create your negotiating tactics. The agent can give you specific information, too, about schools, community services, etc. It's a good idea to request this type of information prior to your interview, so the agent can gather the information for you.

Who Collects and Pays Commissions?

Some buyers think that agents really make the big bucks each time they sell a home. They think the agent gets paid the total commission! You know from reading this book it's not so. Your agent should explain how commissions are divided in his area and office. An example of

---

FIGURE 5.1 • How an Agent Evaluates a Buyer's Potential

After the first interview, the agent evaluates whether a potential buyer is qualified enough to work with him or her.

Rate on a scale of 1 to 4 (4 being the highest).

	1	2	3	4
1. Buyer is motivated to purchase. (Rate each spouse/partner separately.)	1	2	3	4
2. Buyer is realistic about price range expectations.	1	2	3	4
3. Buyer is open and cooperative.	1	2	3	4
4. Buyer will purchase in a timely manner.	1	2	3	4
5. Buyer is a referral source, and will provide referrals.	1	2	3	4
6. The buyer has agreed that he will work only with you.	1	2	3	4
7. Agent has established a positive rapport with buyer.	1	2	3	4
8. Buyer will meet with loan officer.	1	2	3	4
9. Buyer answered financial questions openly.	1	2	3	4
10. Buyer has no other agent obligations.	1	2	3	4
11. If buyer has home to sell, he's realistic about price.	1	2	3	4
12. Buyer will devote sufficient time to purchasing process.	1	2	3	4
13. Both spouses/partners will be available to look for home.	1	2	3	4

As an agent, is this buyer worthy of my time, energy, and expertise?

Adapted from *Up & Running in 30 Days* by Carla Cross, ©1995 by Dearborn Financial Publishing, Inc. All rights reserved.

FIGURE 5.2 • How an Agent Earns His or Her Commission

I'm paid only when you complete a purchase on a property. Otherwise, I'm not paid for the work I do or for any of my expenses. Obviously, then, I want to find a property that fits your needs. I am paid only a portion of the whole commission. Here is an example of how commissions are divided.

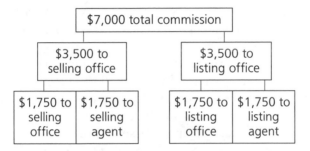

Because my business costs are typically 25 to 40 percent of my gross income, I want to be sure I'm providing customer satisfaction by helping customers find the right home for them.

these divisions is shown in Figure 5.2. You can see your agent won't get that whole commission. Depending on how commissions are divided between companies and within his company, the agent who sells you a home will probably get one quarter to one half the total commission.

In the previous chapter, we discussed various types of representation available to you. If your agent hasn't done so earlier, he will explain these in the consultation. He'll give you choices of representation, and go over who pays commissions. You may be asked, at this point, to sign a buyer representation contract.

Financing Information and Qualifying Guidelines

Your agent can provide mortgage information during the consultation, including loan rates, terms, and programs. He can also qualify you for a loan, or, at least, give you a rough idea of what you qualify for. To qualify you financially, the agent will ask you some questions about your income and your debts, and the amount of money you want to invest as a down payment. Then, using some mathematical guidelines, the agent figures the maximum loan amount a lending institution will approve for you. The agent will tell you what a house payment would be at that loan amount, and can include taxes and insurance and any homeowners' dues. You'll walk out of the session with a general idea of the price of home you can buy, the amount of money you can borrow, and your house payments. Armed with these guidelines, you can start gathering homes to see in the right price ranges.

Some agents love to learn all the new loan programs, and will spend hours explaining them to buyers. Others rely on mortgage representatives, also called loan officers, to qualify their buyers. Agents have access via computer programs to search for mortgage programs and qualify buyers. In fact, about 7 percent of all REALTOR® firms are affiliated with a mortgage network, which provides information on rates and terms, and will prequalify buyers for loans.

How far in the qualifying process should an agent take you? In my opinion, an agent should know enough about financial qualifying that he can give you some guidelines during this initial interview. You and he should both determine roughly the price range of home you can afford. Note: Remember, if you're working with a seller's agent, don't disclose the top price you're ready to pay for a home. Also, you'll discuss the down payment you want to invest, and the house payment you're comfortable with. Or, if the agent doesn't want to qualify you, he should arrange for you to be qualified (or preapproved, as I mentioned in Chapter 2) by a mortgage representative prior to your seeing homes. The agent needs this information to gather a list of appropriate properties for you to see. One of the mistakes buyers make is to find their dream home, and discover they can't afford it. Agents add to this misery, too, by not insisting buyers be qualified for certain price ranges before they haul them around and find them properties they fall in love with.

Ballpark qualifying.   I think it's a mistake for agents to try to be experts at financing, because there are literally hundreds of mortgage programs available, and those change daily. However, I know both buyer and agent must find out, early on, what the buyer can qualify for—and what he's willing to pay. To get a rough idea of that, I created "ballpark" qualifying guidelines shown in Figure 5.3.

FIGURE 5.3 • How Much Home Can You Afford?

With the following two rules of thumb, you can estimate the house payment you can qualify for.

1. Your total payments = ⅓ your gross monthly income

   Your total payments (house payment, plus all your other fixed expenses—car payment, credit cards, etc.) can be a little over one third of monthly gross income.

Example: Your gross income is $4,500/month. Your total payments can't exceed approximately $1,500.

Your situation: One month's gross income = _____
                      × .33 = _____ (all payments)

2. Your total house payment = ¼ your gross income

   Your house payment (including taxes, insurance, and homeowner dues) can be a little over one fourth of your monthly gross income.

Example: Your gross income is $4,500 a month. Your house payment including taxes, insurance, and any association fees, cannot exceed approximately $1,125.

Your situation: One month's gross income = _____
             one week's income   = _____
             (your total house payment)

These are approximate figures. See your loan officer for precise qualifications. With the dozens of loan programs available, you'll want to choose a loan that fits your needs exactly. Your buying power can vary thousands of dollars, depending on the loan program you choose.

The experts on financing.   Where should you get the best information about financing? Go to a loan officer associated with a bank, savings and loan, or mortgage company in your area. An agent should give you three recommendations. If you're working with a good agent, the agent will know who the responsible, competent loan officers and companies are in the area. You can ask your friends who have recently bought about their programs and loan officers. This is the kind of service that's very reliant on the integrity and knowledge of the particular loan officer and company he represents.

Finding the "unbelievable" home loan. Forget it. There's no free lunch. When you're getting a mortgage, you're buying money. Money costs money to get. There are several ways lending institutions make money from you. One is to charge you a low interest rate, but raise other fees, like the loan fee you pay to place the loan. That's why you need a good loan officer who can explain how these trade-offs work. For example, most buyers shop for the lowest interest rate. However, for some buyers, a larger interest rate would be a better choice than a large loan fee.

Insider Secret

☞ The lowest rate or the least cash outlay may not be your best choice.

The best deal. When I was selling homes, buyers would bring me a flyer from mortgage companies I'd never heard of, publicizing great rates. From my experience, I learned these companies can come and go in a flash, and their mortgage representatives can be really slippery. It was difficult, however, explaining why the buyer who was looking for the best deal, shouldn't jump at such an attractive interest rate.

A little trick that some institutions use to increase their profits is to charge you relatively small fees for "incidentals." You have to look closely at your mortgage information papers to see these fees. Although they're usually $50 to $200, they add up. When we bought our last home, we found a "drive-by" charge of $200 listed on the fees the mortgage company said we would owe at closing. I asked our loan officer about the charge, and she explained that a term of the loan was that she drive by our home to inspect the area. Suspect, but, okay. About two months after the home closed, the loan officer called me. She said she had some notes to fill out about the loan. She wanted me to describe the area. I reminded her of that "drive-by" fee, and asked her, since I paid it, hadn't she driven by? Guess not.

How do you avoid choosing the wrong loan officer or mortgage company to work with? Ask for three recommendations from your trusted real estate agent. Your agent knows who the most reliable loan officers and companies are.

Get preapproved. In Chapter 2, I explained the difference between being prequalified and being preapproved. Remember that preapproval means you have been qualified for the loan. All that's missing is information about the property. When you're preapproved, you'll receive a letter of approval. There are conditions in the letter of approval, including that the home you buy will appraise for the amount you paid.

The preapproval letter is your strongest position as a buyer in a competitive market. Mark Warren, one of my agent advisers, strongly suggests you be preapproved before making an offer on a home, especially when you're competing with other buyers for homes. Mark says he's been able to negotiate much more effectively for a buyer when the seller knows that buyer can get a loan—for certain—on his home. When two buyers are competing for the same home, you can bet the seller will choose the lower offer from a preapproved buyer, rather than the higher offer from a buyer who hasn't been preapproved. If your bank's preapproval shows your top loan amount, white it out before your buyer's agent shows it to the seller. You don't want the seller to know you can pay more for the house than you may want to pay.

Does your agent have a team? Many good agents today have tried to streamline the buying process for you by assembling a team—that is, a group of professionals the agent knows and trusts who provide the services needed to process your transactions. This team can include the loan officer, the title company representative, the escrow company representative, the home inspector, and perhaps, an attorney (if attorneys are normally involved in transactions in your area). Because agents can be held liable for the actions of whomever they refer to you, agents are advised to give buyers three recommendations for each member of their teams. Then, you make the final choice. Generally, the members of such a team have no formal business relationship with each other. The relationship is a networking one.

Although it may seem easier for you if you're given only one recommendation per business, don't allow the agent to give you only one recommendation. Sometimes, agents steer buyers toward certain professionals for ulterior motives (more on this in later chapters). Having three recommendations puts you in the driver's seat to make the choices you believe are best for you.

The Property You Want to Purchase

In the consultation, you'll describe to your agent the property you're looking for. In this section, I'll give you tips to discover what you really want in a home, and strategies to ensure that the description you give your agent is right on target, so she can search out the right properties for you. A creative and enlightening way for you to start thinking about what you want in a property was developed by Tim Smallwood, an agent with whom I worked in Seattle. I really like Tim's idea, because it helps buyers capture not only how they want a property to look, but also the "feel" of the place.

First, take a blank sheet of paper. Then, just start writing everything you can imagine about the property you want to purchase. Be as vivid as you can. Describe the look, the sound, and the feel of the property. Write as much as possible. If you're purchasing this property with another person, each person should write his description alone. Then, share descriptions. What's alike? What's different? What could cause dissension? Ask any agent, and he'll tell you that one of the hardest things about showing properties is trying to get both people to agree on any of them! This exercise can save a lot of heartache later.

Basically, describing the house you are seeking can be boiled down to three basic steps:

1. Identifying features
2. Adding the benefits
3. Assessing dominant buying motives

1. Identifying Features

Often, agents use some kind of questionnaire to capture your comments as you describe the kind of property you're looking for. The forms usually stick to the facts—how many bedrooms, baths, square feet, those kind of things. These are called *features*. But, there are many more, different needs buyers want to satisfy with the purchase of a home. These needs go way beyond just the features. Unfortunately, most of those questionnaires used by agents stop way short of what buyers need to think about as they describe the property they want to find.

2. Adding the Benefits

The second step of the process is to figure out why you want those features—what those features will do for you. These reasons are called *benefits*. For example, the benefit to a third bedroom could be privacy for an office.

Let's look further at features and benefits. John and Mary, move-up buyers, want a large kitchen—a feature. What is a benefit of a large kitchen? There are many: storage space, a place for children to play, an area to entertain. The specific benefit depends on satisfying John and Mary's needs. In their case, both are gourmet cooks, and love to entertain. To them, that is the benefit of a large kitchen.

Picture a kitchen. How would one look that was a good place for children to play? Probably not a large cooking area, but with an attached, open family area. A kitchen, however, that satisfied John and Mary's needs would have much more cooking and counter space, and would be open to the sitting or dining area, so they could entertain while they cooked.

You can see how important it is to attach benefits to features. It helps you to narrow your description of the kind of spaces you'll need, and what you want them for. That's the way you and your agent can start really envisioning what sort of property is right for you.

3. Assessing Dominant Buying Motives

The third step is to translate these benefits to our emotional needs, the real motives that cause us to actually fall in love with and buy a property. In sales talk, these are called *dominant buying motives*. These include:

- Security (What will cause you to feel secure financially, safety-wise, etc.?)
- Family security
- Prestige
- Personal space (how you feel about it, not the square feet)

If you've ever listened to people telling you why they bought something, you'll already have figured out that buyers (of anything) make choices based on emotion (their dominant buying motives) and rationalize those choices with facts.

Take buying a car. According to accountants, the most sensible car to drive would be a ten-year-old Chevrolet or Ford. But, how many of us drive that car? And, if we don't, what "facts" did we use to rationalize the car we decided to buy? If I buy a Mercedes, I may tell people that I bought it because a Mercedes lasts so long, and it keeps its value. What really drove me to choose that car, though, was that I wanted to feel I had *arrived*. My dominant buying motive is prestige. Being a modest sort though (well, this is a story), I can't really own up to my prestige motive, so I use the resale value satisfaction to shore up my emotional decision—and to sound mature to those who ask.

If you want to see how creative we can get with these rationalizations, listen to someone try to tell you why he made a decision to get married for the fifth time in ten years. Or why she decided to buy the car that costs $1,000 a tune-up. It's just human nature. We motivate ourselves to buy something because our emotions light the fires of desire for whatever it is we want to buy. Then, so we appear to be adults, we think up some reason to prove that our decision was a smart one. Don't some people make decisions based on the facts? Yes, partly. However, just the facts aren't strong enough in themselves to drive us toward the decision. We need the emotion, too (although many adults won't admit it!).

Let dominant buying motives help you make choices.
We use the same dominant buying motives to drive our decisions to buy cars as we do to buy homes. Again, these are prestige, security (financial, safety, etc.), family security, and personal space. You may have some variations or different names for these, but these are the main categories. A salesperson's job—or your job if you have to do this for yourself—is to translate the features and benefits you say you want into one of these emotional needs.

Here's an example. Let's say, as I question you about what you want in a property, the issue of schools comes up. You tell me you want good schools for your children. Later, you tell me that you must have a safe place for the children to play. As you describe the home you want, you tell me it must have a family room connected to the kitchen, so you can watch the kids (who are eight and ten years old). Obviously, your dominant buying motive is family security. So, when you're looking for a home, you will be happiest with one that makes you feel as though you can provide that family security—even if the home doesn't have some of the other features that you thought you had to have.

Real Life

Buyers are not usually aware that they even *have* a dominant buying motive. After all, no one ever taught them to think about the home they want to buy in those terms. They just describe the features they want in a property. The agent, then, goes looking for properties with those features, trying to keep in mind the buyer's priorities. I learned the hard way that a buyers' descriptions can be misleading. I was referred to Roger and Marilyn, who were being transferred from Cincinnati, Ohio. They had two grade-school-aged children. Roger and Marilyn were excited to move to Seattle, which has lots of big hills, and, thus, views of the territory and the lakes. In our consultation, they told me they were looking for a property with a view in a prestigious area, with good resale value. If you heard the view and area requests, what would you think their dominant buying motive was? Sure. Prestige.

I located some really prestigious areas and spectacular view properties. The day of the tour, I just knew I was going to sell them a home—and soon. I met them at my office, piled them into the car, kids included, and hauled them to the top of the highest hill I could find—one that had breathtaking views of Lake Washington. Of course, what it also had were winding, steep streets, houses perched on cliffs, and few areas for children to play safely. We reached the home I was going to show them. I stopped the car, careful to park it so it wouldn't start for the bottom of the hill while we were inspecting the home. Before I could get out, Roger yelled, "Marilyn don't get out, and, for gosh sake, don't let our children out!" Then, he turned to me and asked accusingly, "Why are you taking us to *this* area?" Luckily, I didn't say that it was because that was what he told me he wanted. Actually, I didn't have the chance, because he kind of beat me to it, screaming this was not at all what he wanted! About that time, I was thinking how interesting it would be to put him on a Big Wheel with the kids and see how long it would take them to reach the bottom of that hill.

After I recovered from my shock, we talked, and I discovered, in his home priorities, a view just went to the bottom of the list. Why? When he described to me what he wanted, he hadn't realized that to get a view in his price range in Seattle, he had to give up flat streets and flat play areas for the children. During this process, we all discovered that a safe play area was much more important to Roger and Marilyn than they had first conveyed to me. Family security was a much stronger dominant buying motive for them than prestige.

Where did they buy? Much farther out, in a new subdivision on an acre (flat, of course), with a great new school. Did I sell them? Yes, but it was touch-and-go there for awhile. Roger felt as though I hadn't listened, and I felt as though he had misled me. Lesson learned: Agents shouldn't take at face value what buyers tell us about their wants and needs. Buyers don't know how to translate these into dominant buying motives—they don't know how to readjust their priorities when faced with the realities of an area. The agent must serve as guide, interpreter, and reprioritizer as buyer and agent go through this process. Hopefully, your agent will know how to interpret features and benefits to uncover your dominant buying motives. Even if he doesn't, you have the information here to discover your own dominant buying motive.

What Did You Say?

Agents have a nasty little saying: "Buyers are liars." Here's what spawned that cliché. When an agent first meets a buyer, he finds out what the buyer is looking for in a home. Armed with that information, the agent dutifully tries to find properties to fit the buyer's description. Then, one day, the agent calls the buyer to make another appointment to see homes, and discovers the buyer has bought a completely different type of property from what he described to the agent! (Of course, he bought it from a different agent, too!) Understandably, the agent feels used and abused. He feels the buyer lied to him. The buyer told him he wanted one thing, and then he bought something else.

Insider Secret

☛ An agent may consider *you* unreliable if you describe one type of property, then buy another.

What's the problem with those buyers? Don't they know what they want? Maybe not, or, at least, they're having trouble describing it. All, in all, though, I don't think the problem lies with the buyers. I think the agent is at fault. When finding out what the purchasers' needs were, the agent didn't ask enough questions—or the right questions. If he had better sales communication skills, he could have asked questions to help the buyer clarify his needs. After all, how can agents blame the buyers when agents are supposed to be the pros in this sales communication process?

Do Agents Listen?

Buyers believe they communicate their property needs clearly to the real estate agent. (They would be shocked to know that agents say "buyers are liars.") The trouble is, from the buyers' viewpoints, the agent doesn't listen. According to buyers, that must be the reason they feel they haven't been shown properties that are right for them. What's going on? Agents think buyers lie and buyers think agents don't listen. Miscommunication. Whose job is it to fix this situation? The agent's. We're talking about developing sales communication skills, one of which is to *listen.* That's why my agent advisory panel suggested you ask your referral source if the referred agent was a good listener. Being a good listener means developing a series of questions that elicit good answers—and knowing how to use those answers as a springboard to get more information.

Now, let's look at the questionnaire you'll use to avoid the miscommunication I've mentioned in the last few paragraphs.

Real Life

Joanne and Bob were moving to Seattle from Kansas. They were starting their own business in Seattle, and, for the past year, had rented a home. Now, they were ready to purchase. I got their feature requirements in a home, and found that they wanted two different things. Bob, a hunter and fisherman, wanted a comfortable home he could relax in. Joanne wanted a gracious, impressive, formal Tudor style home that was prestigious. I found myself running them—and me—ragged, looking for their dream home. Where can you find a comfortable, yet formal, prestigious home? I tried. One day, as the three of us were returning from a long trek down the freeway to see a builder's homes, Joanne told Bob that she really had to have an impressive brick Tudor in a certain prestigious area. Bob shot back, "Joanne, I don't know why you want such a nice home. You never keep house in the one where we live now!" I wanted to press the "eject" button on my car (if I had one) and just pop out.

What a clash of dominant buying motives! Bob wanted security, and Joanne wanted prestige. What did they settle on? A comfortable home with lots of storage for sports equipment (no Tudor, no brick) in a prestigious area. Then, I didn't know how to determine buyers' dominant buying motives. So we three just had to feel our way through the process. Oh, if I knew then what I know now, I could have spared them some painful confrontations—and spared me from observing them.

The Home Information Form

Figure 5.4 is the questionnaire I've been referring to in this section on finding appropriate properties. The questionnaire is different from most because it leads you to describe not only the features but the benefits you'll want from the property. Take storage, for example. What kind of storage do you need? What's it for? My husband is restoring a 1947 Chrysler Windsor convertible, and three quarters of the garage has been used for the past few years as storage for the car and its parts. Well, I'd say three quarters, he'd say one half. (Do you know how *big* those 40s cars were?) So, when Dick says "storage," it has a certain meaning—now—to me. It has a little different meaning to him. (Can you tell we've had disagreements about how the rest of the garage should be used?)

As you look through the questionnaire, take the time to really spell out exactly what you want that space for. Then, compare your needs with any partners in the purchase (spouse, friend, etc.). You will get some stunning surprises! That's good. Now's the time to get surprised, not after you fall in love with a particular home and discover your partner hates it.

Do both of you want to move? Here's a loaded question in the questionnaire: Moving will accomplish—what? I've worked with couples where one spouse wanted to move and the other didn't. That's a tough position for an agent to be in. I strongly suggest, if the person you want to purchase with is not as excited about purchasing as you are, that you sit back for a moment and reflect on what would happen if you did find a home you love. To have a good buying experience, both buyers must want to move, with about the same intensity.

Evaluating the Agent

During the consultation, you should ask your questions from Chapter 3 to evaluate your agent. When should you ask them? After the agent has completed the home information form and has given you the information you want. Sometimes, the agent may suggest you and she go out on a trial tour, and then decide whether you want to continue working together. If that's the case, ask your questions when you return from the tour, and before you go any further with the agent.

A Marriage Not Made in Heaven

At the end of the consultation, a good agent will ask you for a commitment to work with him exclusively—to be loyal to the agent. He may ask you to sign a buyer agency contract. What if you don't want to

FIGURE 5.4 • Home Information Form

Exchanging this information prior to seeing properties will help you find exactly the right property. In addition to relating the physical requirements you want in your desired home, this questionnaire will help clarify what's really important to you—your lifestyle and values that impact the home you want to purchase.

Family Information

Name _____ Date _____ Source _____

Address _____ Phone _____ Office Phone _____

Number in family _____ Children _____

Name _____ Age _____

Name _____ Age _____

Name _____ Age _____

Husband's employer _____ Wife's employer _____

Reason for moving _____

Leisure activities/interests _____

Will someone else be helping you make your purchase decision? ____

If so, who?_____

Locations

Preferred school districts _____

Preferred areas—describe feeling/look of area _____

_____

Homes seen in area that you liked _____

What kept you from purchasing? _____

Previous work with agent? When? _____

FIGURE 5.4 • Home Information Form *(Continued)*

Time Frame

How long have you been looking?_____

What's the reason you haven't purchased? _____

Desired date of possession _____

If we found a home now, could you purchase? _____

Home Features

_____ Resale   _____ New   _____ Bedrooms   _____ Baths

_____ Family room/describe how used _____

_____ Rec room/describe how used _____

_____ Basement/describe how used _____

_____ Kitchen eating space _____ Hardwood floors _____

_____ Fireplace locations _____

_____ Garage/workshop. Describe _____

_____ Place for hobbies. Describe _____

_____ Boat parking/storage-function_____

_____ Storage. Describe _____

_____ Other considerations/use of _____

Home Style

_____ Two-story   _____ Multi-level   _____ Other

_____ Split   _____ Tri-level

_____ Rambler   _____ Daylight rambler

FIGURE 5.4 • **Home Information Form** *(Continued)*

Why is this style important? _____

_____

Home Setting

_____ Acreage. Function _____

_____ Privacy. Explain _____

_____ Trees   Open/sunny _____   Garden_____

_____ Neighborhood. Describe _____

Other considerations _____

_____

Overall home/setting feeling _____

_____

Moving will accomplish _____

_____

Present Home

Do you need to sell your home to buy?_____

What do you like the best?_____

The least? _____

Is your home presently listed for sale?_____

Would you prefer selling your home prior to buying?_____

How did you find your last home?_____

_____

Services you found valuable that an agent provided _____

_____

FIGURE 5.4 • Home Information Form *(Continued)*

How much equity? _____   Market analysis needed?_____

Other origins of down payment? _____

Future Investment

_____ Price   _____ Initial investment

_____ House payment   _____ Terms

Do you know how much you qualify for?_____

---

commit yourself to that agent? First, decide whether you just don't want to work with that agent or whether you want more time to consider that agent. If you are unsure of the agent, and have some unasked questions, ask them now. Do not commit to any agent if you're not sure you want to work with that agent. Remember, any agent can show you homes. You're looking for services way beyond that level.

If you want time to think over your mutual commitment, just tell the agent that you want a few days to think it over. If, after the consultation, you are sure you don't want to work with the agent, tell the agent at that time. You can just say that you don't think the partnership will work. If pressed for your reasons, you can either give a specific reason, or, if you're more comfortable, just say it's how you feel. You don't have to give a reason. It's your choice.

What You Will Have Accomplished in the Consultation

I believe the consultation is the single most important step in the buying process. In most cases, you'll be making your final choice of real estate agent during the consultation. And, that's the most important decision you'll make during this process. What you accomplish here greatly determines the success of your buying effort. I think you'll agree the objectives of the consultation are really important. This meeting is the only way I know for you to complete these objectives.

Here's what you will have accomplished in that consultation. In the meeting, you gathered the information you need to calm those anxious feelings. Now you don't feel you may be getting yourself into more than you bargained for. You're actually excited and positive about looking for the property that's right for you. For the first time since you thought about buying a home, you have more answers than questions. You got information about the homebuying process, loan programs, were qualified for a home price range, and discussed appropriate properties, price ranges, and areas. All that real estate lingo is even starting to sound like it belongs in the English language.

Using the Home Information Form in Figure 5.4, you've been able to provide the agent with a clear description of the property you're seeking, including the features you want and the benefits the property will provide. You've even gone further than that. You've identified and prioritized your dominant buying motivators, the emotional needs you must satisfy to make the right decision. You've compared features, benefits, and dominant buying motives with your buying partner, and have agreed on some compromises, because you two discovered you had two different dominant buying motivators in mind. (Comparing, compromising, and agreeing on priorities will make the process of seeing and weeding out potential properties much more enjoyable.)

During the last part of the consultation, you used the agent questionnaire from Chapter 3 and qualified your agent. After evaluating her answers, you decided to work with her. She will be representing you as a buyer's representative, so you'll be her client. You've signed a buyer's agency contract, clarifying the terms and conditions of her employment. You and she have agreed to meet to see homes a week from the consultation, which gives her time to preview properties and pick the most appropriate ones for you. In the next chapter, I'll show you how to identify your preferred "buying style," and use the information to keep your buying process on track.

Frequently Asked Questions

Q. I really like an agent I met in an open house. When I mentioned the consultation, she said that wasn't necessary. What do I do now?

A. If you're really compelled to continue with this agent, ask her why she doesn't use the consultation. Ask her how she will provide the information listed in this chapter. Then, if you're satisfied you're getting value from her, ask her the qualifying questions in Chapter 3. From proceeding with buyers both ways, with and without a consultation, I much prefer the consultation approach. Otherwise, it's too easy for me to miss something that later becomes important to the buyer.

Q. I met an agent at a party, went to look at a home with the agent, and fell in love (with the home). However, the agent didn't call me back. I've placed calls to his office, and he doesn't return them. What should I do?

A. Either call his manager and find out where the agent is, or choose another agent. Personally, I have a very low tolerance for agents who don't return their calls. If it were me, I'd get some referrals of competent agents and choose one of them.

Q. We met an agent at an open house and asked her some questions. We weren't satisfied with the answers and decided we didn't want to work with her. When she called us later, we told her we didn't think our working together was a "good match." I thought she would take the hint. However, she's called again four times. I don't know what to say to get her to quit calling. Help!

A. The next time she calls, explain you are interviewing other agents. At this point, you have chosen not to work with her. If you change your mind about working with her, *you will call her* and arrange an appointment with her. Ask her *not* to call you. That should do it!

6

The Psychology of Homebuying
What You Need to Know

*W*hen buyers start looking for homes, the stress level goes up. Yes, it's true buying a home is a big financial and emotional decision. Worries about money and heightened emotions are certainly enough to elevate stress. But, those aren't the only reasons blood pressure rises, tempers fray, and friendships (or marriages) become unraveled. Much of what causes human beings to act like savage animals when they buy a home comes under the category of psychology. Knowing why we're behaving differently and what to do about it, can keep the stress levels manageable. In this chapter, I'll address the following aspects of the psychology of homebuying:

- The work of locating a home: setting reasonable expectations for length of search; number of homes seen; and the amount and type of work you'll have to do
- The psychology of the sales process: identifying how you like to work through it
- Your behavioral style: pinpointing your decision-making preferences

I think much of what causes stress is "free-floating" anxiety. We're always anxious about the unknown, so we worry, we fret, we let fear freeze us into indecision. Not knowing what's going to happen makes us block future plans. But, give us facts, figures, and a process, and we can envision a bright, positive future. Our anxiety level drops, and we start looking at the unknown as an exciting adventure. Then, we'll get into action and accomplish what we said we wanted.

Gaining insights in the three areas in this chapter will unblock your vision. It will keep you from indecision and help you stay focused on your goal: Buying a home.

The Work of Buying a Home

Don't kid yourself. You can't find a home you want to buy without some effort—in fact, some significant effort. In this section, I'll give you some guidelines on how long you should expect it to take to find a property, how many properties you'll probably have to view, and how much work you should be prepared to do. I'll also prepare you for some psychological feelings you'll have if you find a home "too quickly" (at least, if you think you made a decision too quickly).

How Long Will It Take to Find the Property You Want?

According to the NAR, buyers take, on average, 15 weeks to find a home. But, that's like saying the average family in the United States consists of one and one-half children. Sometimes, a buyer can look at three homes, and decide one of those homes just exactly suits his purpose. Other times, a buyer can look for years.

Insider Secret

☞ Buyers who are certain they've found the "perfect property" probably haven't!

Don't look forever. During my eight years as a salesperson, I sold hundreds of homes. A big mistake I saw buyers make was to look for too long. If you can't find a home to purchase within six months, you're probably trying to find the "perfect" property. You're the type of buyer who has made a four-page list of all the features you must have. You're the kind of buyer who tells the agent, "I'll only move if I find exactly what I'm looking for." Every time you see a home, you haul out that list and start checking off the features. You get more and more frustrated, because there's not one home—not even *one,* that has even half of the 342 features you must have. Quit that right now! I know, from building a custom home, there is no perfect home, even if you think so when you design and build it yourself. Why? Your needs change, your lifestyle evolves, and your children grow up.

While you've been running yourself ragged for ten months searching for all those features, a home that would fit your needs has come and gone. Some savvy buyer has snapped it up, is taking advantage of the tax write-offs, and enjoying actually living in the property! So, take some advice from an observer (me) of frustrated buyers: Don't focus on an exhaustive feature list! Raise the priority of the property site and surroundings and the area amenities. Pick the five features you just must have. Envision the possibilities for improving the home's features to your specifications. Remember, you can enhance the features in a home (for instance, by adding a bedroom), but you can't really change the home setting or the area. Identifying your dominant buying motive, discussed in the last chapter, goes a long way toward freeing you from the tyranny of trying to find a home with the right 342 features.

Don't become a professional "looker." Agents have a term for the buyer who loves to look, but never makes a buying decision: The "looky-loo." Agents find this person easy to identify, because he knows more about the properties for sale in the area than the agent does! What the agent also knows is this person will likely never buy a home. Looking at homes and engaging agents in conversation has become an avocation.

Here's an observation from one who's watched dozens of home-buyers keep themselves in indecision. I think some buyers really don't want to buy a home. That's why they have those four-page feature lists. I think what they find fascinating about the homebuying process is seeing properties and evaluating them. They love to compare properties with their features lists. They tell their friends how hard it is to find their perfect home. They don't know they're cleverly avoiding making a buying decision by rejecting every property.

If you find yourself becoming a "looky-loo," get together with your buying partner and your agent and decide whether you just may not want to buy a home now. That's fine. In another year, you may have a different frame of mind. Don't waste your time and your agent's, if you really don't want to buy.

How Many Homes Should You Plan to See?

Buyers moving long distances look at more homes (22), on average, than all buyers (18). Many variables determine the number of homes a buyer sees. The transferee, for instance, may never have been to the area. He must see the areas where he might like to live, and get a sense of the kinds of house styles, price ranges, and community amenities available. The transferee sees so many properties so fast that he's well educated, though exhausted and confused.

On the other end of the spectrum is the casual "looker" who lives in the area. Every weekend, she visits open houses. She becomes well educated—and until something changes in her life, not very motivated to do anything with all the information she's gathered. Finally, she decides to move. By then, she's decided on the area, the home style, the price range, and the amenities. Sometimes she'll look at only three or four homes before making a buying decision.

Don't confuse yourself by viewing too many homes too fast.   Another mistake I see buyers make is they try to see too many homes in a day. Transferees, especially, see so many properties they can't remember the ones they said they liked!

Plan with your agent to view properties no more than three hours in any day, and see no more than five properties at one time. (These guidelines depend, of course, on the areas you must cover to see those homes.) If you're transferred, you'll have to spend any free time you have available. Just try not to exhaust yourself. Remember, after you've seen more than five properties at a time, they all start looking alike—and none of them look special!

How Much Work Will You Have to Do?

Homebuying, my agent adviser Karyn Sandbeck observes, is a second job for a buyer. You'll need to dedicate some serious time and effort to the homebuying process. Talk to your agent about the best time for you to look at homes. For many people, that's Saturday morning or Sunday afternoon. See if you can schedule two or three blocks of time, about three to four hours each, for the next few weeks, so you and your agent have a real plan of action. If the market is hot, you'll need to be ready to roll when your agent tells you about a property that's just become available.

When only one buying partner inspects the properties. What happens if one of the buying partners takes the responsibility of inspecting dozens of properties because the other partner just doesn't want to look? Here's an example of what happens: John and Mary have discussed moving. Mary says she's willing to move, but she wants John to find the best three properties, or maybe the best property, and she'll okay the purchase. Now, this sounds pretty good in theory. John, who is really motivated to find a new home, dutifully makes the list of features and benefits he wants (and he thinks Mary wants). He sets the appointments with the agent, and, for weeks, inspects properties and narrows the field. When he picks his favorite property, Mary will inspect it and give her blessing for the purchase. Problem: John has become educated and realistic about the properties available, while Mary is blissfully unaware of the property situation in the area. So, when John excitedly shows Mary the property he chose, Mary finds 23 reasons why this property just won't work for them.

What's really going on here is a little game I call "gotcha." Mary didn't really want to move, and she's going to be sure none of the properties John finds will fill the bill. If your buying partner doesn't want to become educated about properties by seeing them, you're going to have a problem when you try to get a decision from your partner. Remember, it's work to find, evaluate, and narrow the field to the property you want to buy. Much of this work is really about educating yourself. The only way both buying partners can make a good decision about a property is to have gone through this educational process together.

The Psychology of the Sales Process

Think about the last time you bought a car. Start from the beginning of the process. Remember the time when you first became conscious of the need for a different car. What got your attention? What happened to start you thinking about trading your car for a better one? Then, how did you proceed? Maybe you gathered information about various cars you thought you might like. You talked to your friends. You visited a car showroom. The more information you got, the more interested you became in purchasing a different car. You started noticing problems in your old car—problems you had previously tolerated. Now, they seemed to increase, convincing you that you need a new automobile. As you narrowed the field of choices, you got more excited about driving a spiffier model. The problems with your old car, coupled with the desirability of the new one, really motivated you to make a buying decision. Finally, you found just the car, and took action to purchase.

I've just described the stages each one of us goes through before making a buying decision. We go through these every time we make a decision, whether we're purchasing season tickets to the symphony or buying a new home. These four stages make up the sales process:

1. Attention
2. Interest
3. Desire
4. Action

In this section, I'll explain the steps in the context of purchasing a home. Understanding the psychology of the sales process will help you identify where you are at any point as you buy a home. It will help you evaluate whether you're making progress, or getting stuck in one part of the process. Stress and conflict can occur when one partner gets ahead of the other in the sales process. Knowing how to get back in step not only can make the buying process more pleasant—it can save a relationship!

1. Attention

As I write this book, it's December, and the stores are decked out in holiday finery. The display windows in the clothing stores sparkle with the lights of the season; inside, the mannequins show us spectacular party attire of beads, feathers, and velvet. What could be more enticing? Those display windows are eye-catching so they rivet our attention. If we hadn't thought about buying something new for the holidays, we probably will when we see those displays! The retailers intimately understand the sales process. They know they must help us take the first step, to get our attention, if they are to sell us something.

From unconscious feeling to conscious thought.
Let's go back to that example of making a buying decision about a car. You're driving a ten-year-old car and appreciate it drives well and is

paid for. It has a few rattles, but you've grown to appreciate them as part of the car's character. One day, though, your friend drives up in the niftiest new set of wheels. You take the car out for a spin. It's fun, fast, and doesn't rattle. A few minutes later, you jump in your ten-year-old beauty. For the first time, the rattles annoy you. They seem to have gotten worse. You start thinking about trading the car in. Now, you are moving toward *attention* in the car buying process.

In the homebuying process, this attention step may be as simple as deciding, on impulse, to drop in on that open house one Sunday. Reading the newspaper ads, too, may focus your attention on buying a home. Now, the idea of moving has become conscious. As you start into those open houses, your attention is focusing on the possibility of purchasing a new home.

When are you in the attention phase of homebuying? When you start seeing more open house signs than you ever noticed before; when you start reading newspaper ads; when you start talking to people who just bought homes. When you're in the attention phase, is it possible to buy a home that day? Not likely, unless you can take yourself through the rest of those steps very quickly.

What happens if you are in the attention phase and your buying partner just doesn't want to pay any attention to the possibility? Seeing homes for sale is a good way for your buying partner to focus his attention on buying. You may find that no matter how much you talk about purchasing, no matter how many homes you drag your partner to, you just can't get his attention. What that means is the partner just won't get motivated to go through the buying process. You can't force someone to start through the sales stages if he doesn't want to make the journey!

2. Becoming Interested in Making a Move

To start the pursuit to get what we want, we must become *interested* in the product or service, and what it will do for us. To continue the process toward purchasing a home, we must become personally engaged, interested, and excited about the possibility of gaining a new home. If our motivation wanes during this time, we decide that what we thought we wanted to do just wasn't worth it. For instance, we know we should lose weight. We see an ad on TV that gets our attention by showing a person who lost 50 pounds. Our interest goes up when we find, for only $29.95 per month, we can buy the diet product advertised. Then, the phone rings, and our best friend tells us he's getting a divorce. We forget all about the diet program, and focus on our friend. Although the product got our attention and a little interest, the interest wasn't sustained long enough for us to continue the buying process.

Who gets you interested in the possibility of your purchasing a home? It could be an agent, questioning you about your needs. It could be your friends moving to nicer homes. It could be just plain necessity—being transferred or having another baby. It could be that you feel owning a home would ease your tax burden. Having a competent agent who keeps asking us questions can keep us focused on the goal, and on not becoming demotivated about purchasing. And, conversely, a good agent will sense if it's *not* the right time for you to purchase, and tell you. How does the agent know? By determining that you are not interested and motivated enough to feel taking the risk to purchase is greater than the risk of not purchasing.

How do you know you're in the interest phase? You are gathering information about homes. You're watching the Sunday TV home show. You're visiting open houses. Your present home starts looking less desirable. To sustain your motivation for a different home, you should keep reminding yourself of the benefits you'll gain with the purchase.

What will kill your interest? Thinking of all the negatives involved with purchasing. Deciding it's just too much trouble. Having a buying partner who doesn't want to buy. Working with a real estate agent who doesn't help you find benefits, or who doesn't give you enough information at this stage.

3. Stoking the Fires of Desire

By the time you reach the third stage, *desire,* you are really becoming excited about the benefits of this purchase. You have discovered your dominant buying motive, and have seen a property that fulfills your emotional needs. Remember, the motive or emotion drives the decision, not the facts. It's very important that you are able to remind yourself of the benefits of this property now. Because, on the opposite side of the coin, you can be demotivated by fear. You're afraid of higher payments, more responsibility, and the unknowns that go with purchasing a home: moving, making financial decisions. Sometimes, this fear becomes general free-floating anxiety, paralyzing us from making a decision that we know would benefit us.

How do you know you're in the desire phase? You really want to buy that home. You're feeling really good about purchasing and excited about moving into that property.

What can kill the desire? A buying partner who doesn't want to make a decision. An agent who tries to rush you into a decision. Or, an agent who holds you back from a decision! Can you kill your own desire? Sure, by bringing up every worse-case scenario you can think of that might happen if you purchase. The desire phase, too, can be very strong, but fleeting. I've seen buyers back away from buying a property that would have been wonderful for them, because they talked themselves out of it. Knowing where you are in these sales steps, and how your reactions might help or hinder you, will help you recognize when the time is right for you to go ahead and take action.

4. Getting into Action

Finally, we're ready to take action, to purchase. To complete this step, we must balance the fears with the benefits until the benefits outweigh the fears. When you are in the action phase, you make a decision on that home and you create an offer to purchase it.

How quickly should you get to the action stage?
Would you think something was wrong if you saw two properties and decided to buy the second one? Not if you had taken yourself through the sales process to *your* satisfaction. Some of us are able to make decisions quickly. That is, we can move through the buying steps quickly. Others of us take much longer to make decisions. It all has to do with our natural style and what we've learned by making decisions in our business and personal environments.

Getting in sync with your buying partner.
Maybe you're buying by yourself. If not, you should be sure you and your buying partner are going through the sales stages at the same pace. When you and whomever you're buying with go through the steps at the same time, it's a pleasant experience. It doesn't work so well when you're not going through the steps at the same pace. Let's say one of you has looked at homes for six months, gotten all excited about one, and dragged the other party, unprepared, to the home. One of you is ready to buy and one of you hasn't even gotten to the attention step! The person who hasn't even thought about purchasing feels as though

you would if you left work after a grueling day, ready to unwind, and, instead, had to go to a rip-roaring party in full swing. Out of it. That person can really fight your enthusiasm.

Here's what to do to get you both in step. Knowing the sales process stages, you can identify which step you're in and where your buying partner is. Then, you'll need to help your buying partner through the steps preceding yours, until your partner catches up. You can do this by seeing and reviewing homes you've seen, and reviewing the Home Information Form you completed in Chapter 5. Also, sitting down with your agent to review where you are in the buying process is helpful. Remember, when people feel as though they're being pushed into a decision, they push back. Help your buying partner relax and get the information needed to keep moving through the steps.

Getting in sync with your agent. You've been looking for homes. You're ready to buy. You walk into an open house and fall in love with it; you tell the agent hosting the open house you want to make an offer. (I'm writing this as an example. Yet, I hope that you know better than to do this after having read this book!) The agent, whom you've never met, is totally unprepared for your "desire." He's thinking he has to get your attention. You get really antsy, because you're ready to buy, while the agent is making chit-chat. You wonder why the agent isn't listening to you! I call it the out-of-sync syndrome. This time, the agent is the one who dropped into the party that was already in full swing.

Here's another reason for you to choose your agent before looking for homes. If you've been working with a competent agent, he can identify where you are in the sales process at any given time, and help you *there*. I hate to think of all the buyers, ready to buy, who have been squelched by an agent who didn't recognize where the buyers were in the buying process.

The pushy agent. One of a buyer's biggest complaints is that agents are pushy. What's really going on is that the agent is focused on "action," while the buyer is at the interest step. Some unskilled (or, at worst, unprincipled) agents seem to operate always at full-throttle. They ignore the first three stages in the sales process, and try to force buyers into the last one, action, before the buyers are ready to act. The result is that buyers feel the agent doesn't care about their needs. He wants only the money. Many times, that's true. Sometimes, though, it's just that the agent doesn't know any better.

Understanding the sales process, identifying where you are in it, and recognizing where you may be getting stuck, is important, for these insights help you lower your and your partner's stress levels and control your buying experience.

Your Behavioral Style

The last psychological element in the buying process is your behavioral style. From studying actions of people, especially when they're under stress, psychologists have identified four basic behavioral styles:

1. Analytic
2. Driver
3. Amiable
4. Promoter

Each of these behavioral styles has a favored way of reacting to situations and making decisions. For some examples, see Figure 6.1. Knowing your behavioral style can help you control your stress levels during the buying process. You'll have insights into the following:

- Why you prefer going through the buying process in a certain time frame and process
- How you tend to act under stress, and how you like to make decisions
- How your buying partner likes to make buying decisions and tends to act under stress
- The behavioral styles you're most compatible with, and those that naturally cause you conflict
- The behavioral styles with which your partner is most compatible, and those that naturally cause him conflict

In this section, I'll explain the four behavioral styles, help you identify yours and your partner's, and give you a "heads up" so you can avoid potential conflicts with your buying partner and your agent during the decision-making process. Let's begin by looking at each style in Figure 6.1.

FIGURE 6.1 • **The Four Behavioral Styles**

Analytic	*Driver*
Car: 10-year-old Chevrolet	Car: Black Mercedes
Wears: Clothes she's had for 20 years	Wears: Power suits
Works: Boeing or Microsoft	Works: Doctor or CEO
Decisions: Tons of information/ takes a long time	Decisions: Fast; just the facts
Balances checkbook: Daily	Balances checkbook: Someone else does it
Amiable	*Promoter*
Car: Older Volvo	Car: Red sports car
Wears: Eddie Bauer	Wears: Red and gold
Works: Nurse or teacher	Works: Salesperson
Decisions: Takes a long time, must have lots of support	Decisions: If it "feels" right, pretty fast
Balances checkbook: Carefully	Balances checkbook: Never

The styles that are situated diagonally from one another in Figure 6.1 are least alike. As you can imagine, these two styles have the most style clashes, causing conflict, when purchasing a home. As you read the descriptions that follow, pinpoint your style and that of your buying partner. Working with the strengths and weaknesses of each style, you'll be able to anticipate style conflicts when it comes to making a decision about a home.

The Dictatorial Driver

Think of a profession that requires lots of decisions—fast. Management is one of those. People in management typically are what the psychologists term "drivers" or "high aggressives." This type of person wants "just the facts, ma'am." He doesn't like small talk, and certainly doesn't like looking at any more properties than he has to. Also, since drivers are used to making lots of decisions quickly in their professions, they are kind of in practice for making quick decisions.

Here are some indicators that you are a driver: You are or would like to be in a business where you're in charge. You may be a doctor, an attorney, or a manager. You wear serious businesslike clothing, no flashy duds. You drive a powerful, heavy car. You give orders rather than asking lots of questions. Your favored way of dealing with others is "My way or the highway." Are you that type, or do you know someone who is?

Drivers must watch out for being too impulsive when making decisions. Sometimes they don't gather enough information. Also, they can bully a less aggressive partner into making a decision too quickly for the partner. Drivers may need to slow down and pay more attention to their partner's feelings. Drivers should also watch that they're not too impatient with a partner who wants more information—even though drivers never do!

The Agreeable Amiable

Look at Figure 6.1 again. Diagonally across from the driver is the amiable. These are people who are nurturers, like nurses and social workers. They aren't pushy or driving, and take longer to make buying decisions. They also don't like pushy salespeople. What's a pushy salesperson to an amiable? Anyone who wants the amiable to make a buying decision faster and differently than he feels comfortable.

The important word to the amiable is *feel*. The amiable needs to feel supported in his decisions. He's also the type of person who gets "buyer's remorse"—the depressed feeling that can occur right after you've decided to buy a home. The amiable second-guesses himself about every decision, and many times will talk himself out of a decision. He's the one who calls the salesperson late at night after purchasing a home and says he thinks he made a mistake. (More later on this in Chapter 11.)

How can you tell if you're an amiable? Your work lets you nurture and care for others. You are patient and empathetic, so much so that sometimes people take advantage of you. You prefer sensible, casual clothes (never flashy) and drive a safe car, probably a four-door sedan or stationwagon. You are drawn to homes and areas that are just like your clothing—sensible and middle-of-the-road.

To avoid conflict, your buying partner needs to support your buying process all the way through, and not push you into a decision. You must, however, watch out for becoming wishy-washy, and putting off making a decision.

The Promoter

A real "people" person, the promoter is the one wearing the latest fashion getup and driving the flashiest car he can afford. The promoter makes decisions reasonably quickly, and bases his decisions on how he *feels* about everything—the area, the salesperson, and the property. He's the guy who wants to know who lives in the area—(he likes to feel like he's "arrived") and what the home looks like on the outside (appearances are important). He doesn't want lots of facts—they could confuse his feelings! You might think of a promoter as an amiable on steroids.

What kind of businesses are promoters in? Sales, marketing, and show business. My husband is a typical promoter. For years, he was a radio personality DJ, spreading his inimitable warmth and humor via his voice and personality over the airwaves. If Dick likes you, never mind the facts. He can always find some way to rationalize them, anyway. He makes his judgments about people based on how he feels about them.

If you're a promoter, watch that you don't try to charm your buying partner into making the decision you want. You're a good salesperson! You may be willing to skip over the facts, but your buying partner may not be able to make such a leap. Watch, too, that you get enough hard information to make a good decision. You're too good at selling *yourself* on what you want, and ignoring the negatives at times.

The Analyzer

Diagonally from the promoter is the analyzer. This person just can't get *enough* facts—and doesn't even trust them if anyone gathers them except *her!* Common professions for the analytic are engineering and technology. She dresses very conservatively and drives an older car. (Chances are she's had the clothes and the cars for a decade, and they're perfectly functional.) She has had the same hobbies for 30 years. She's very reliable, and keeps the same friends for life. Guess how long the analyzer takes to make buying decisions? Sometimes, so long that the properties she wants to buy have been bought and sold a couple of times!

The style most in conflict with the analyzer is the promoter. If you're an analyzer, you will hate to "be sold," either by your buying partner or by the real estate agent. You'll frequently feel you're being pushed into a decision too quickly (you'd prefer to gather information indefinitely). You'll need to watch that you're not putting off a decision by saying you must gather more facts, simply because you're afraid to make a decision. Set a time line for yourself, with deadlines for your decisions. If you feel pushed by your partner or a salesperson, sit down and explain where you are in the buying process, and list the information you need to make a decision. Agree on the time when you will be ready to decide. Otherwise, you will really drive your buying partner or salesperson up a wall. Can you imagine what happens when both buying partners are analytics?

When Stress Levels Go Up

As tempers fray and buyers and agents tire, stress levels go up. Higher stress causes buyers and agents to act even more "like themselves." That is, the buyer who's a driver will scream directives. The analytic buyer will ask for more information, and then discount it so the decision is put off. The promoter buyer will try to charm away the facts, or act as if someone has hurt her feelings. The amiable buyer will stall and complain that no one cares about him. Staying in touch with yours and others' behavioral styles can defuse situations that cause buyers (and agents) to "move into their corners" of their behavioral styles—where their worst attributes intensify, and result in style clashes and confrontations.

Style Clashes with Your Agent

In this section, I've given you insights into your style and potential conflicts you may experience with others' styles. I've provided tips so you can anticipate style clashes to eliminate conflicts that can ruin a buying experience. Don't think that agents will be able to help you with these style clashes. Not many agents use the behavioral style principles to counsel buyers or adjust their own styles. Some of the comments from buyers prove my point:

- "That salesperson was just too pushy." (A driver salesperson and an amiable buyer)

- "That salesperson wasted our time showing us properties we didn't want to buy." (An amiable salesperson and a driver buyer)
- "That salesperson just didn't keep in touch with us." (An analytical salesperson and a promoter buyer)
- "That salesperson tried to force us to make a decision too quickly." (A driver salesperson and an analytical buyer)

If reading this above hasn't given you a headache already, just think about how selling situations can become more complicated. Add in another buyer or two—with different styles from their buying partners. Now, let's make matters even more complex. We'll have a seller or two (or more), and another agent (or more) involved as we start negotiating. So, you can see, understanding behavioral styles can be very helpful in anticipating any style clashes—both with the agent and between buying partners.

Armed, Forewarned, and Prepared

With the knowledge about the psychology of buying a home, you're ready to get out into the field and find the home of your dreams. Remember, buying a home is as much a mind game as a physical one. Stop, look, and listen to what's going on between the personalities as well as what's happening in the real estate market.

Frequently Asked Questions

Q. I'm a driver, married to an analytic. I hate buying something that costs more than $1.95, because my husband takes so long to consider the buy that I've lost interest. How can I get our buying styles more in sync?

A. Gather loads of information to help your husband make a decision. Give him a reasonable deadline for a decision. Ask him lots of questions and listen carefully to his answers. Ask him to gather more facts. Then, relax and slow your process down.

Q. I'm an analytic and my wife is an amiable. The agent we're working with must be a driver, because every home we see, he asks us to buy. I'm getting sick of it! I told my wife how irritated I was, but she said not to rock the boat. How can I get the agent to respect our buying timeline?

A. If you're working with a driver, you can't be subtle. They don't get it! Tell the driver *directly* not to ask you to buy each home. Instead, tell him you will be happy to go back to the office after each home tour and summarize each home, prioritizing each home's interest to you. Give the agent a timeline, too, for your decision. In this case, you must drive the driver—and get him to slow down!

Q. My husband and I are both amiables. Every agent we've met seems to be too pushy for us. How can we find another amiable to work with, who will understand our needs?

A. Unfortunately, there aren't many amiables selling real estate. Why? They're so nice and respectful of people's feelings they back off from helping buyers make decisions. They're so supportive that they let buyers and sellers walk all over them. Still, there are agents selling real estate who combine the best attributes of the amiable (sensitivity and supportiveness), with the requirements of a salesperson who actually makes money—to help people make decisions, and be firm when required. Seek out a friendly, yet businesslike agent, and explain how you want to work. Realize, too, that three amiables together might really appreciate each other and never come to a decision!

7

Locating Properties

$\mathcal{N}$ow that you understand the psychology that's going on while you're starting to look for properties, let's delve into the property search itself. There are five common ways buyers find properties they may want to see:

1. Rely on real estate agents to search for appropriate properties.
2. Read the newspaper advertising and call for information.
3. Drive by homes and call real estate companies listed on the signs.
4. Visit public open houses on weekends.
5. Locate them on the Internet.

In this chapter, I'll tell you the pros and cons of each of these methods, and what to watch out for as you use each method to locate properties. As you start to search in earnest for properties, you'll have to sort out how properties are priced. I'll explain two different methods of pricing properties today, tell you who really prices those properties, and give you tips on how to use pricing to sort out the properties you really should see.

FIGURE 7.1 • Informational Sources Relied Upon

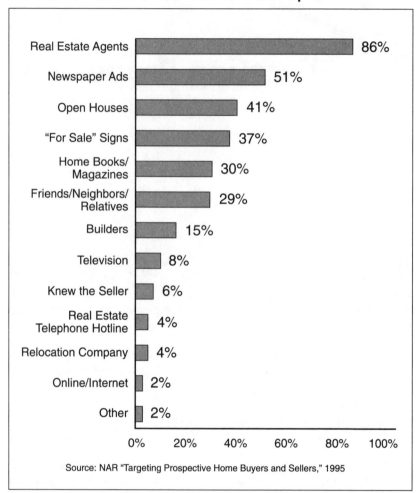

Source: NAR "Targeting Prospective Home Buyers and Sellers," 1995

Most Buyers Find Information about Properties from an Agent

Figure 7.1, results of a study from the National Association of REALTORS®, shows how buyers got information about available real estate properties. As you can see, the vast majority of buyers (86 percent) got their information about properties from real estate agents.

If you've had a consultation with a real estate agent by this time, and have agreed to work with an agent, having your agent research appropriate properties is by far your best choice. Why? Because you have given a detailed description of the kinds of properties you want to see. Your agent has access to property information and knows the territory, and can sift the good from the bad—and the downright ugly. The agent can save you lots of time you could spend running down properties that aren't what you thought they'd be. Also, your agent can get the latest in property listings from her multiple listing service—the instant the property is available to agents in the area. In addition, large companies have intranets, and/or Internet home pages just for their agents. They post their new listings even faster than they are listed on the multiple listing service.

Searching for Properties on Your Own

As you can see from Figure 7.1, buyers rely on other methods besides real estate agents to find potential properties. Some of these methods can cause buyers to get really frustrated when they take searching for properties into their own hands. For instance, print advertising like you see in newspaper ads, is designed to create better-than-life descriptions of the properties. As you'll see in this chapter, the descriptions usually don't fit the realities. Not only that, but as I discussed earlier, agents use ad calls to try to entice the caller to become the agents' clients (or customers, depending on the agency relationships established). I'll give you pointers in this chapter to avoid those manipulative sales tactics.

Other property sources are a little more reliable than print advertising. When buyers call a real estate company because they saw a sign in the yard, at least they have seen the exterior of the property and the neighborhood. The best of these sources is the public open house, because the buyer can see the neighborhood, the exterior, and the home interior. But, spending all your time traipsing through open houses to get property information is not the best use of your time. You can't know the price or terms before you see the home (unless you've circled all the ads, made a tour map, and dutifully followed it every weekend). So, you're doing lots of work to screen properties that would never fit your needs. Again, manipulative sales agents use open houses to pull some pretty clever sales tactics on buyers. I'll warn you what to look for and avoid in this chapter.

Now, let's look at each of the "on your own" property sources in depth.

Print or Pictorial Advertising

As shown in Figure 7.1, newspaper advertising is the second-largest source for property information, after real estate agents. Other forms of print or pictorial advertising, in order of their popularity with homebuyers, are

- homes magazines,
- builders (probably builders' ads), and
- television shows.

All of these sources give you the same breadth of information. Because you can see nothing, or little, of the home or area, there are limits to the reliability of the information they provide.

Let's look at what happens when you search for properties through newspaper ads. You're going to call on ads, because you're the kind of person who feels you can get the job done better than anyone else. You haven't taken my advice to choose a reputable agent, or you just feel you can find newly listed properties faster than your agent. Let me burst that bubble right now. It takes three to ten days from the time an agent places an ad in the newspaper to the time it actually appears. There's even a longer lead time for homes magazines. But, it takes only one day for the agent to place a new listing in the MLS and have it available for all member agents. An agent can locate newly listed properties faster by far than you can.

You're still going to read the ads, because you want to educate yourself. Before you start, you need to know why real estate agents write ads: To make the phone ring. How do agents get that phone to ring off the hook? By making the home sound better than it is! If you want to test my statement, just drive through a midpriced residential area. How would you describe, in writing, the homes? Now, go read the paper. How are those same homes in that same subdivision described? Do the homes sound like those you saw?

Insider Secret

☞ If the property ad reads too good to be true, it probably is.

Newspaper ads aren't written to sell the advertised home. Did you know that very few buyers actually buy the home they call on? According to studies I did in both of my real estate offices, less than one percent of our sales were from buyers who called on an ad and actually bought that particular home. So, why do sellers love to have their homes advertised? They think buyers call on an ad, see the home, and buy it. Ads do serve a purpose for sellers and real estate agents, though. Ads supply buyers for all listed homes. A buyer calls on an ad. He sees the home, and doesn't like it—naturally. But, the agent has another home to show him. The buyer sees that home—and loves it. It's kind of a "bait-and-switch." Agents advertise one home. Agents sell you another.

My advice is don't fall for it. Just get the information and give it to your agent, who can check the property with his information sources. Here's my opinion: Calling on advertising is a waste of your time, if you have a competent agent.

Property Signs

The next most common method of finding properties is to cruise the neighborhood and call on yard signs. The good news about property signs is that you can have seen the property and the surroundings. You have more reliable information about the property than you could have gotten from reading an ad. But if you're going to call on property signs, be sure you take notes on each property you view. It's easy to become confused about which property goes with which phone number! Before you call, note the area amenities. Drive through the area and note any other property signs. Call on those, too, to get a sense of the price ranges in the area.

As I told you in an earlier chapter, agents use property sign calls to get customers, just like they use ad calls. I'll give you the same advice as on ad calls: Tell the agent you're calling that you've already chosen an agent. Then, gather the information the floor person gives you about the property, and turn the information over to your agent to research further.

Open Houses

As you saw from the REALTOR® survey, 41 percent of buyers used open houses to gather information. And you'll recall from Figure 2.3 that 8 percent of buyers actually chose a real estate agent because they met the agent at an open house. You're going to avoid choosing an agent just because she's at a home you walk into (unless you also qualify the agent using my qualifying criteria, of course). Your objective in viewing open houses is to gather property information. Here are some things to look for:

- Comparable pricing—How does this home compare with others you've seen?
- Condition—Does the home seem to be in comparable condition to others priced like it? Does it seem to be in the kind of condition you want?
- Area price range—Does it fit into the price range of the area (for a good investment, it shouldn't be much higher—or lower—than the prevalent price range of the area)?
- Room sizes—Are the room sizes adequate, and comparable for homes in its price range?
- Amenities for its age—Does the home have amenities comparable to homes of its age, like type of woods and finishes? Has it been remodeled or updated? Does it have newer appliances?

When you're inspecting homes, take along the Property Checklist in Chapter 8. Take information about the home, available in the open house. After you leave, make notes, so you'll remember the specifics (it's easy to get confused if you see more than five homes in any given day).

Insider Secret

☞ You probably won't find the home of your dreams by walking into an open house.

Will you walk into the home of your dreams?

It's fine to educate yourself about the market by visiting open houses. Just don't think that is the way you'll probably find the home you want. In fact, studies I did at my real estate offices showed that less than 3 percent of buyers purchase a home they visited at a public open house. Why? If buyers like the home on the outside, it's probably too costly! Also, what we see from the outside may not fit our needs at all.

If people don't buy the homes they visit on Sunday, why do sellers insist on agents holding them open and advertising them? Sellers don't know what you know—that very few homes are sold as a result of holding them open. If they knew, they wouldn't be so disappointed when they come back home at 6:00 PM on Sunday, and excitedly ask the agent, "Did you sell it?" when the agent says "no." The next question from the seller is, "How many people came through?" The agent hems and haws, and finally says "two" (that's counting the curious neighbor). So, the seller is really mad at the agent. The seller prepared for that open house for a week! Then, the seller had to figure out where to go to get out of the house for three hours on Sunday. To add insult to injury, only two people came through.

Why, you ask, would an agent set up a situation where the seller would be mad, and the agent didn't sell the home? Some agents just don't know that very few homes are sold at open houses. Most do know, though. They don't tell the sellers, because, like floor time, agents use this marketing method to "pick up buyers."

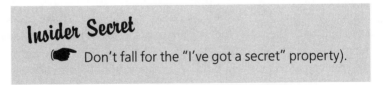

Insider Secret

☞ Don't fall for the "I've got a secret" property).

A manipulative sales technique to avoid at open houses. In Chapter 2, I mentioned the slippery sales techniques listing agents use to entice you to buy properties while visiting their open houses. Here are a couple more variations of the "fear" sales tactic they use so well. As you visit open houses or call on ads, you may run across a manipulative sales technique from an agent, which goes like this: "This property is available only through me. If you want to make an offer on it, you must choose me as your agent." A variation is, "The sellers have asked us not to expose the property to other agencies yet. We're the only ones you can buy this property through." An even more sophisticated one is, "Since this property is available only through our agency, if you make an offer now, you won't have any competition."

When you hear these lines, you panic, and think, "Well, I guess, to get the information on this property, I must work with that agent." Wrong. In every area, there are rules created and enforced by the local MLS to make sure that all properties listed by their members are available for viewing by all members. Generally, the rules state that the listing agency has 24 hours to provide the MLS with the information. (Check with your agent about the "exposure" rules in your area.) Yet this rule is broken every day, as agents refuse to share their new listings with other MLS members. Why? If the listing agent can sell the property himself, he makes twice as much money. This is an excellent example of "self-agency"!

There's a lot wrong with this practice, both legally and ethically. Let's say you're a seller, and you're listing your home with an agency who's a member of the MLS (and almost all sellers list with an agency so affiliated). You're paying a healthy fee, and you're paying it because you want your home exposed to all the agents—fast. You know that more agents bring more buyers, meaning more competition for your property. The agency who listed your home has agreed, as a member of the MLS, to abide by the rules. The agency also has promised the seller, legally, through its fiduciary relationship, to market the property to all MLS members—fast. Sad but true, though, is that some agencies and agents let their greed drive their businesses. They even have a line of patter to convince the seller that it's *not* in his best interest to expose the property to an additional 10,000 agents (rather than their 70 agents). I'll admit, you've got to be some kind of a salesperson to convince a seller that exposing the property to many less agents is a better idea—for the seller!

Insider Secret

☞ You can buy a property from any agent *you* wish to use—or employ.

Be sure you have representation. You've been told you must purchase that property from that particular agent/company. That's simply not true. You can buy that property from anyone you please who is licensed to sell real estate in your state. If you're pressed by "buy now," stop the conversation with the listing agent. Immediately call your agent; if she's not available, call her broker. Have your representative call the listing agent. If he won't give your agent information, have your agent immediately call the broker. If your agent then can't get information, have your agent's *supervising broker* call the other broker. If all else fails, have your agent call the seller directly (check with your agent about the rules and practices of your area). As a last resort, call your department of licensing. You have a right to buy a property promoted by any member of the MLS agency from the agent of your choice.

Locating Homes on the Internet

There's one other method buyers use to search out homes, and it wasn't available five years ago. Today, you can preview homes for sale around the world—just by turning on your computer, logging on, and visiting Web sites that specialize in real estate. Some of the most useful sites for you will be those of your local real estate companies. Their Web sites are listed in their advertising section of the local newspaper. In addition, some national sites are

- Realtor.com (http://www.realtor.com)
- Home and Land Magazine (http://www.homes.com)
- HomeScout (http://homescout.com)
- The Living Network (htp://usa.living.net)
- International Real Estate Directory (http://ired.com)

These and more sites are listed in the "Other Helpful Sources" section of this book. Many real estate sites provide all kinds of buying information along with showcasing listed properties.

As you can see from Figure 7.1, very few buyers are using online sources now. However, that number is growing by leaps and bounds. Not only that, it's the thing to do for some buyer groups, especially the so-called Generation X. This group, born between 1963 and 1977, doesn't want to be "sold." They want information, and they know how to find it using technology. They're computer-literate and don't want to contact a real estate agent until they've done some background research. If you're in that group, you'll enjoy surfing the Net to educate yourself.

Insider Secret

☞ Not all the properties you see advertised on the Internet are still for sale.

Check the property information for accuracy.

It's easy to get misinformation on the Internet. This is particularly true about properties listed on the Net. Some of the properties you might see listed on the Internet are no longer available—or no longer listed with that particular company. Some real estate companies don't update their listing inventory on their sites very often. When I was managing my last real estate office, I found that one of our listings was featured on a competitor's site. I looked up the listing, and found that the competitor had the home listed eight months earlier, but we had been the listing agency for the past three months. So, I called the competitor to ask what was going on. The owner of the firm patiently explained to me that they just hadn't gotten around to taking the listing off their site. After all, he explained, it was good for his business to get calls on the property.

If you call on a property, see the property, and note that the property isn't listed with the firm who answered that ad, the price, terms, and conditions of the property may have changed from that earlier listing. If I were you, I wouldn't deal with the agency who misled you with a home advertised as listed by them. That's a bad way to get started in a professional relationship. Instead, take that information back to your agent and let your agent research the home and show it to you, if it's appropriate.

A note to Generation Xers: I know you like to get information, and, if you're a first-time homebuyer, you're wary of real estate agents. Remember, though, at some point, you'll be using a real estate agent to purchase a home. Take the advice in this book: Choose a real estate agent early in your information-gathering process. Let that agent sort through the information you've gathered, acting as your purchasing consultant and partner. That way, as you gather property information, you'll avoid manipulative techniques agents use to capture you as a customer or client. Why? Because you already have an agent who's acting as your buffer and adviser.

This advice goes for all you buyers. Remember, your real estate agent is the best source for property information, and the best person to prioritize the information you gather by yourself. Using your agent this way gets your money's worth from your agent, and protects you from manipulative techniques and misinformation.

The Ins and Outs of Property Pricing

As you look at properties, chances are you'll be baffled at the pricing. While some properties seem priced well, most don't. In this section, I'll show you how properties are priced, including a new twist, the "range" pricing technique. I'll tell you who actually sets the price you see listed, and how to evaluate listed prices as you get ready to make your offer. Armed with this information, you can sort the wheat from the chaff. Of course, you'll be relying on your agent to give you his professional insights during this part of the purchasing process.

How Agents Determine Value of a Property

There are two ways agents determine pricing on properties today: The specific pricing approach, when a price of a property might be listed at $160,000, and the range pricing approach, where the property would be listed in a price range, such as $160,000 to $200,000. In this section, I'll show you how each works.

Specific valuation. When I started in real estate over two decades ago, it was common practice to merely "eyeball" a home and tell the seller a price—that is, just walk through the home, ask the seller a couple of questions, and give a price off the top of your head. The "eyeball" method of pricing a home is very uncommon today. Now, an agent does lots of research to figure out what a property is worth. This research is compiled into a comparable or competitive market analysis, a study of properties comparable and competitive to that of the seller's property. The market analysis is made up of three types of information:

1. Comparable homes that have sold and *closed.* (That means the buyer made an offer on the home that was accepted, the buyer

completed the transaction, and the seller received the money due him from the sale. The home now belongs to the new owner, and the public records show the new owner, along with sales price.) Homes that have been sold and closed are regarded as the most reliable indicators of home value.

2. Comparable homes presently on the market for sale. (Because sellers can place any price on a home they want, this is a less reliable source for value, as you'll see in this chapter.)

3. Comparable homes whose contracts to sell have "expired." (After their properties have been listed a while, usually a period of three to six months, sellers get frustrated that their homes haven't sold and take their properties off the market. Agents say a listing whose contract period expires before the listing is sold is an "expired" listing. The expiration of a listing indicates that the seller wanted more for the property than buyers were willing to pay.)

Why are all three categories used to price property? First, only the homes that have sold and closed are proof of what buyers were willing to pay for properties. However, when the seller puts his home on the market, he also must compete with similar homes that are presently on the market. Seeing how these homes are priced is another piece of the puzzle in accurately pricing property. The expired listings indicate a "too high" range of pricing.

Market analyses are done today with the help of computers, which allow agents instant access to public records and MLS records. Information from all three categories is pulled together and collated to create a thorough study. Agents use computer software programs to arrange the study so it looks graphically pleasing—and very official. However, accurately pricing a property is as much art as science. Merely gathering information, collating it via a software program, and coming up with a price just doesn't ensure correct pricing.

Some agents are great at pricing properties, combining both experience and talent. They use their brains as super-computers, factoring in such variables as the home's condition, decor, and site placement; attractiveness of that block or street; schools; community amenities; and terms of sale. All these variables must be weighed.

It is important to know how market analyses are prepared for seller's pricing. As you'll soon find out, many properties aren't priced properly, and some of this poor pricing is a result of relying on too many "for sale" comparables, and not enough "sold" comparables. In addition, knowing how a market analysis is created is really important when you make an offer. If you have a buyer's agent, your agent should do the same kind of market analysis for you when you make an offer on a home as the seller received when he listed his home. Then, you'll have confidence that your offer is backed by the value of the property.

A new twist in pricing properties: range pricing.

Until recently, all properties were listed in the multiple listing service with one specific price, like $198,950. Now, there's another way to price properties—range pricing (this practice has various trademarked names). Rather than just give one price, a range of prices is listed in the property information. The same property that would be listed as $198,950 might be range priced at $190,000 to $215,000. That means the seller would look at any offer in that range.

Why real estate companies started range pricing.

As real estate companies' expenses escalate, they've looked at all kinds of strategies to reduce expenses and raise profits. One of the biggest expenses companies and agents have is marketing listed properties. If marketing time can be shortened, the dollars spent promoting the property can be reduced. Some bright real estate professional came up with a solution to shorten the number of days a property stays on the market, and get more sales: Offer buyers a range of value for a property.

Generating more buyer interest in listed properties is really important in a "slow" market, a market where there are many more properties available than sales, a market where properties stay on the market for more than six months. So, range pricing is used primarily when properties are selling slowly. In a hot market, range pricing all but disappears.

Buyers' viewing and buying habits encourage range pricing.

Here's the psychology behind range pricing. Agents know buyers generally won't look at properties priced much beyond what they want to pay. In fact, they get angry at agents who show them properties priced above what they said they wanted to see. However, agents know many properties are overpriced and should be viewed and considered by buyers looking in lower price ranges. How do agents, then, show buyers a wider range of properties, to encourage more offers? By using a vehicle such as range pricing that tells buyers it's okay to look at higher-priced properties, and it's okay to make lower offers than they would have with specific pricing.

Here's how range pricing works. Let's say the seller wants to list a property at $200,000, which the agent feels is 20 percent more than the property is worth. Listed at $200,000, the buyers who would find the property attractive (the $160,000 buyers) will never see it. Why? Buyers don't want an agent to show them properties out of the price range they can afford or want to pay. But, the seller insists that he "wants to start there," pricing his property at 20 percent over what the listing agent feels will get showings.

Seeing that the seller won't accept listing his property at the agent's recommended price, the listing agent then introduces the concept of range pricing. This allows the seller to get the best of both worlds: He gets to try a higher price, but signals the buyer that he's willing to see offers in the listed price range. To decide on a range of price, the agent does a market analysis and recommends a range of price that encompasses the high end of possible pricing, and the lowest price the seller will accept. The property will be listed in the MLS, both at the $200,000 price (to be in accordance with MLS rules), and at range pricing; in this case, let's say the range is $160,000 $200,000.

What range pricing has done is encourage buyers to look in wider price ranges than before, and to make more offers. What's the downside? Listing agents don't have to be as good at pricing properties. The responsibility of figuring out what the property is worth has shifted from the listing agent to the buyer's agent and buyer. Is this bad? Not if you have a competent buyer's agent, and you educate yourself in range pricing. However, if you're going to make offers on your own, or don't have a competent buyer's agent, you are at a disadvantage if range pricing is being used in your area. Have your agent explain the specific practices of range pricing in your area, so you can look at the right price range of homes, and make the right kinds of offers.

Setting the Listing Price on a Property

Both specific valuation and range valuation are used to determine listed prices. However, the price that you see advertised on a property may not be the result of a market analysis. It may be the whim of the seller! Although agents make recommendations for pricing, the seller finally decides on the price at which he wants to market his property. Most sellers want more for their properties than the listing agent thinks is appropriate. At that point, the agent must make the decision to list the overpriced property, or walk away from the property. Unfortunately, agents too many times decide to list the property at the seller's price—a price that is too high to attract buyer showings and offers. In the next few paragraphs, I'll discuss why agents take overpriced properties, and what this means to you as you try to figure out property values.

How many properties are priced to sell fast?

As you view homes, you'll start drawing conclusions about what properties fit certain price ranges. However, you'll also see that some properties seem not to fit the price category you would imagine. That's because properties are priced in wildly disparate ways. Sometimes the owner just insists on a certain price. Sometimes agents put a high price on a home just to please a seller. A minority of properties are priced using statistics.

What indicates that a home has been priced correctly? It sells within a reasonable amount of time for close to full listed price. Most sellers—and even buyers and real estate agents—think that *all* homes with For Sale signs in front of them sell *sometime.* That is not the case. Here is what happens over a six-month period to all the properties listed during that time:

- Only about one third of the homes you will see actually get a "sold" sign on them (within half a year).
- About one third of the homes you may see will never sell. They'll become "expired" listings.
- Another third of the homes you see will still have For Sale signs on them long after you have made a choice of home (they're so overpriced that chances are you will never be shown them).

These figures were taken from the Puget Sound area's MLS. Your agent should provide you with the figures from your own area, if they're available, so you'll know the ratio of sales to listings available in the area. Of course, these ratios change as the market gets slower or faster. If the market heats up, you'll find more homes selling faster, because buyers are desperate to find a home, and are competing with other buyers.

Why agents list overpriced properties.

Agents get paid only when a property sells and closes. If only one third of the properties listed sell in reasonable market time, why would an agent bother to list the property if he knew he couldn't get paid? You might think an agent just doesn't know the right price for the property, and innocently places too high a price on the property. Once in a great while that's true. However, with the computer programs and property information available today, that's not often the case.

Here's how properties end up overpriced. Usually, the agent knows the right price for a property but can't convince a seller. After all, sellers understandably want every penny possible for their property. They're afraid they'll underprice their homes, and "leave some money on the table." They don't trust the price the agent gives them. Most agents, afraid to lose the listing, just agree to list the home at whatever price the seller wants. Then, the agent figures that he can get the price down later (and maybe use the property to pull the old bait-and-switch on unsuspecting buyers).

You can see from the statistics that this strategy of overpricing doesn't work very well to get properties sold. Once sellers list a property at a high price, they think the property will sell. When they get few buyer showings, they blame the agent. Instead of lowering their price, they insist the agent provide more ads and open houses. Finally, they get frustrated with the agent and list with another company. Sometimes, they list with three or four companies over a period of a year or two, holding out for their high price, insisting that agents spend more marketing dollars, concluding that the real estate industry is just unable to sell properties. (That's true. No agent or company can force buyers to pay more for properties than they feel is a good value!)

How to deal with overpriced properties. As you see properties, your agent will give you feedback on right pricing (if you have a buyer's agent). You will learn quickly when a property is priced well—and when it's not. You will instruct your agent not to waste your time showing you properties that are overpriced—unless you and your agent decide that property is a candidate for a lower offer. (More about that later in this book).

Deciding What Prices to Include in Your Properties to Inspect

Buyers don't want to see properties out of the range they can purchase. However, as you've seen in this chapter, many of the properties available are overpriced. If you restrict your agent to a narrow price range, you may not see the right properties. There may be an overpriced property available whose seller would accept a low offer. When you and your agent are deciding which properties to view, here's what I suggest. Ask your agent to compile a list of properties that fit your needs, regardless of whether they are in your most desired price range. As you discuss these properties, your agent can advise you if she thinks there's some chance of your buying the property for less. If you find a property you like that is more expensive than you can or want to buy, strategize with your agent on a lower offer. That way, you'll see the right homes. In the next chapter, I'll provide tips on how to structure your offer.

Being the "Model" Buyer (or, How Not to Drive Your Agent up a Wall)

I hope I've convinced you to keep control of your buying process by referring other agents you meet during your property search back to your agent. This simple rule will save you time, money, and effort. One of the things that drives agents nuts is when a buyer keeps getting pulled away from a good buyer-agent relationship by unscrupulous agents who use some of the manipulative sales techniques I've warned you against. Buyers are especially susceptible to these sales spiels as they search for properties. There have been times when I wanted to blindfold a buyer and stuff cotton in his ears to keep him from listening to the creative sales spiels of other agents. Remember, those other agents don't want a lasting business relationship with you. They want a commission—now. They will tell you anything you want to hear to sell you a particular property. Don't fall for it.

Besides refusing to fall for those manipulative sales techniques, there are a few other ways you can be a model buyer, and get the best from your agent. I'm sure you want hard work, loyalty, and honesty from your agent. To get that, you must give loyalty and honesty back. I have had buyers who fibbed to me about their finances, their seriousness in buying, and whether they were being loyal. Yet, they would be furious at me if I treated them that way. You just can't expect your agent to go to the ends of the earth for you, if your agent doesn't trust you. If you feel you can't tell the truth to the agent, get another agent! You want your agent thinking you're the best thing since sliced bread. When your agent goes to the seller to negotiate, you want your agent saying glowing things about you—and they'd better be true!

It's okay to evaluate your agent using the insider secrets I'm sharing in this book. But, once you've decided that agent is trustworthy, treat the agent as your partner. You will get the best from your agent, from information to negotiation to a lasting business relationship. It's literally worth thousands of dollars in your bank account for you.

In closing, let me give you the six behaviors of a model buyer:

1. Be open and express yourself clearly, so your agent can do the best job for you.
2. Give the same respect and courtesy to your agent that you expect from him.
3. Be on time for your appointments; if you need to cancel, do so in plenty of time, so your agent can put the time to use.
4. Do your homework and paperwork to prepare for your showings or to move the transaction along to closing.
5. Be realistic about your needs; you may want your dream home, but the homes you see available are the reality.
6. Be loyal. You're in a partnership; if you have chosen your agent well, your agent will be there "for life," not just during the transaction.

Frequently Asked Questions

Q. My agent and I got together to create a tour of homes for me. I've heard that Mercer Island is a great place to live, but my agent hasn't included any homes on the island. Why not?

A. If Mercer Island is a very high-priced area, it could be that the best values for you won't be found there. Ask your agent why she hasn't included the island. Ask to see a few examples of homes in your price range in that area. Sometimes, agents do forget to include a wide range of possibilities for the first tour. Many times, though, the agent knows you'll be disappointed in what you can buy on Mercer Island.

Q. I won't be working with a buyer's agent. How can I get the pricing history you mentioned so I know if the home I'm interested in is a good buy?

A. Go the county clerk's office and search county records. You can find the price the owner paid and when he paid it. You can also find other home sales in the same area to compare with the listed property.

8

Narrowing the Field to Make the Best Choice

You've interviewed and chosen an agent; you've decided what kind of home and neighborhood you're looking for; and you've identified your decision-making style and dominant buying motive. You've worked with your agent to locate properties you want to see, and have taken into consideration the pricing strategies I explained. Now, you're ready to look at properties—inside and out, to make a good buying decision. In this chapter, I'll outline a simple system for you to keep track of the properties—and to keep your agent on track.

Organizing Your "Buying Adventure"

If purchasing a home is a second job, it makes sense to create a system to organize the process. Here are the three areas you'll want to organize:

1. Information about the homes you see
2. Evaluating and inspecting the homes
3. Narrowing the field to make a choice

Gathering Information about the Homes You See

As you tour homes, you'll be picking up information on each of the homes you will view. This information may be a computer printout, a hard copy of the information in the MLS book (if still used in your area), or a flyer from the home, promoting the property. As you tour the properties, keep a running list of the homes you see and organize the information you get according to the tour's organization. Use the Property Checklist in Figure 8.1 to evaluate each of the properties you see. Make enough copies for each of the properties you'll evaluate.

Summarize and review after each tour. If you're like most buyers, you'll probably look at several properties before making a buying decision. These properties may be very similar. Without a method for summarizing and remembering what you saw, you can easily start confusing the features of one property with those of another. So, after each tour, go back to the real estate office and sit down with the agent. Review each of the properties you saw and prioritize them. Decide which ones are still in the running, and which ones are not. Keep the paperwork on the "in the running" properties in one folder. That way, you'll stay focused on what you want and assist your real estate agent in searching for other appropriate properties.

Seeing the right properties. One of a buyer's main complaints about agents is that the agent didn't show him properties he wanted to see. Some of this may be the buyer's inability to accurately describe what he wants. Frequently, however, it happens because the agent didn't have the sales communication skills to ask the right questions. It may be the agent's inability to translate what buyers say they want into the properties available on the market. If you feel you're not seeing the properties you want to see, tell your agent *directly*. Agents aren't mind readers. My agent advisory group sounded a little frustrated when they told me they didn't think buyers spoke out enough. So, voice your opinions, loud and clear. A good way to do this is to sit down with your agent and review your Home Information Form, introduced in Chapter 5. Look at what you said you wanted. Compare that with the properties your agent is showing you. What's out of "sync"? As you looked at properties, you may have changed your parameters subconsciously. Reviewing what you said before you started looking for properties is a great way to get back on track. Here are some tips to help you see the right properties:

- On your first tour with your agent, don't plan on seeing the home of your dreams. Your first tour should be viewed as an educa-

FIGURE 8.1 • Property Checklist

Use this grid to keep track of the properties you'll see. At the end of the tour, we'll recap these homes to decide which one(s) fit your needs.

Home A:_____

Home B:_____

Home C:_____

About the house:	Priority	A	B	C
Price				
Real estate taxes				
Water bill				
Heating bill				
Electric bill				
Age of house				
One-story				
Two-story				
Wood frame				
Brick and wood frame				
Aluminum siding				
Overall exterior condition				
Storm windows				
Garage (note capacity)				
Gas heat				
Electric heat				
Hot-water heat				
Age of heating plant				
Central air-conditioning/age				
Number of bedrooms				
Living room				
Separate dining room				
Kiitchen eating area				
Number of bathrooms				
Closets				
Refrigerator				
Cooking stove				
Disposal				
Dishwater				
Clothes washer/dryer				

FIGURE 8.1 • Property Checklist *(Continued)*

Laundry space				
Adequate water heater				
Basement storage area				
Finished basement				
Attic storage area				
Finished attic				
Number of fireplaces				
Drapes				
Carpeting				
Modern electrical wiring				
Sump pump/drainage				
Overhead sewer system				
Backyard patio				
Fence on lot				
Pleasing landscaping				

About the neighborhood:	Priority	A	B	C
Streets clean				
Neighbors' property well maintained				
Flooding (check local government)				
Loud noises, bad odors				
Nearby train tracks				
Open drainage ditch				
All utilities installed				
Area zoned residential				
Nearby industry				
Proposed special assessments				
Garbage collection				
Streetlights				
Streets and alleys well maintained				
Heavy airplane traffic				
Newspaper stories about community or school difficulties				

The house is near:	A	B	C
Public transportation (within walking distance)			
Thoroughfares or expressways (short driving time)			
Convenience shopping			

FIGURE 8.1 • **Property Checklist** *(Continued)*

	A	B	C
Schools the children will attend (check school officials)			
Parks			
The house is _____ minutes from:	A	B	C
Work			
Downtown			
Convenience shopping			
Elementary school			
High school			
Doctors			
Relatives			
House of worship			

tional tour, where you look at several areas, price ranges, and home styles, so you can get a sense of the territory. Let the agent use wide parameters in designing the tour.

- After the agent has gotten your reaction to this broad range, narrow the field. You won't miss out on a home or area that you would have loved, if your parameters had been larger.

Looking in the next higher price range. Al Johnson, one of my agent advisers, observes that the homes that look best to buyers are the homes just out of their range (or what they want to pay). If you are not seeing what you want to see, ask your agent what the next higher price range is like (if it's at all in your ability to buy in that price range). Go on an investigative tour to see if your dream home is in the next price range up. If you can afford to purchase in this range, at least you know that your dream home exists. Also, perhaps you can make a lower offer on a property that fits your needs. After seeing that next price range up, you and your agent can decide either to change your price range parameters, or change your home specifications. Remember, though, not to be too narrow in your price ranges. Surprising but true: For every thousand dollars you pay, it increases your house payment only about $10 per month! Sometimes, looking at homes priced only $5,000 higher can find you your "ideal."

Nothing available? If you have named very narrow search parameters, your agent may tell you there's nothing available. Although your agent thinks she's doing exactly as you want, she may be listening to you too literally. There are hundreds to thousands of homes available to purchase in every area. There's a strong possibility there is a home for you. It may be in an area other than the one you specified. It may be up one price range from what you've considered; it may be different physically than you described. I think many buyers miss opportunities because agents just don't ask buyers to expand their parameters. If you hear "there are no homes available," look at the parameters you've given your agent. Sit down and discuss your needs again with your agent, and attempt to expand the price, area, and style parameters.

Seeing all the properties you *want* to see. Earlier, I told you that buyers, on average, look at 18 properties before making a buying decision. There are still some agents who don't want to show this many properties. They're operating in an outdated and, in my opinion, manipulative manner. They show three or four homes, and try to "close" the buyer (force the buyer to make a buying decision) on each home. Their philosophy is the more buyers they can close fast, the more money they can make. They don't much care about establishing long-term relationships; those just get in the way of their "numbers game." These agents even have a pattern of showing. They'll show you three overpriced and/or beat-up homes and, finally, one great one. You get the picture. They're not showing you homes to educate you; they're showing you homes to "close" you. If you should find yourself in this situation, I recommend that you discuss the issue with your agent. If you still feel as though your agent is a "closer," not an educator, sever your relationship with this agent and find one who wants something more than a quick sale.

Insider Secret

☞ For some agents, the motto is "show four and close the door."

146   B U Y E R   B E W A R E

You will be buying the home and the neighborhood. Before you get serious about a property, observe what's going on in the neighborhood. Who lives there? If you have children, are there other children in the same age group? Do you see any evidence of people "hanging out"—people you wouldn't want hanging out around your home? Do you see any old cars parked in front of the homes—cars that look like they couldn't move under their own steam? Do you see refuse piled by a few of the homes? What about the yards? Are they well kept, or unkempt? Do you sense that the residents are making improvements on their properties, or letting them go in disrepair? You can easily draw your own conclusions just by driving through the neighborhood and observing.

What agents can't tell you about the area. When it comes to giving buyers information about neighborhoods, agents must be careful not to be discriminatory. For instance, let's say an agent knows the neighborhood you're interested in has a majority population of a different race from yours. When you ask about who lives in the neighborhood, the agent may be tempted to show his superior judgment and knowledge. So, he tells you that you wouldn't "fit into the neighborhood" or "you wouldn't like this neighborhood." Those comments are illegal, because they "steer" buyers toward or away from neighborhoods. Agents can give you facts of public record, but are not to make any judgmental or opinionated comments. These are fine lines, and agents must avoid any semblance of making illegal statements.

Don't ask your agent to provide judgments about the neighborhood that could be interpreted as discriminatory. You can do a thorough investigation by getting county and city statistics. You can visit the local police station, pick up crime statistics, and talk with the local police. You can visit the local schools and get information about specific programs. There are programs available to agents that provide some of these statistics. I just received in the mail a new program on CD-ROM called *Know the Neighborhood*. It gives a map of the area, a neighborhood snapshot, community facts, public and private schools, housing transactions, crime rates, climate reports, houses of worship, and community amenities. Ask if he has access to that kind of product. I've listed some of these products, too, in "Other Sources of Information," at the end of this book.

Real Life

I was a new agent, and, like most new agents, was eager to work with *anyone* who said he wanted to buy a home. I got a request from a young couple, first-time buyers, for a "fixer-upper" on five acres, for $20,000. Excitedly, I told them I would start looking right away. I drove hither and yon, and just couldn't find anything livable (for humans) on five acres for $20,000. When I told the young couple that $20,000 wouldn't buy five acres and something livable, they thought I just hadn't looked enough. Why? Because, in the counseling session, I didn't show them what $20,000 would buy. I should have taken them on a preliminary tour to show them general price ranges. I hadn't learned that an agent must educate a buyer about price ranges *first,* before promising to search for something that may not exist. (I learned, through the years, most new agents make the same mistake.) Because about 20 percent of all real estate agents have been in the business less than one year, you can imagine why buyers think agents just don't listen. In many cases, the agent just doesn't know that the ideal as described by the buyer—doesn't exist—for *real.* The end of this story is that the couple bought a small home on a city lot—from another agent.

I unwittingly misled buyers as a new agent. At least, through that experience, I learned that I had to tell buyers, during our first home tour, we'd be looking at general price ranges and areas, to see the real—what properties look like in certain price ranges and locations. That way, the buyers could reconcile what they wanted to buy for a certain amount with the prices sellers were charging for the real thing.

Evaluating the Properties

By now, you've gathered information on price ranges and neighborhoods, and you're viewing good properties. You're using the Property Checklist to remind yourself of the properties you like. Here are some tips on evaluating and inspecting the properties you find may fit your needs:

- Try always to enter the home from the front entry, so you get a sense of the home layout.
- Take your time as you look at the home. Try to imagine the home without any furniture, because you're buying the home, not the decor (usually). I've seen many buyers reject a good home because of puce wallpaper or furnishings that were much different than theirs. Almost everyone who buys a home changes something after they move in. You will too. Use your imagination to envision how you could make this house your home.
- Open all the closets and doors.
- Be sure to look at the garage and storage areas.
- As you look at the yard, ask yourself if you're willing to do the kind of yard work that particular property requires—or will you change the landscaping?

What needs to be fixed? When you make an offer on a property, you will ask for an inspection. However, you should observe homes you're interested in with an eye to condition while you're touring those homes. After all, the inspector won't say in his report that the bedroom needs painting. But, if you move in and find out later that you need to paint the interior of the home to be comfortable there, you'll have added costs and time.

It's easier to see things that need to be done than you think. For instance, one area of concern is the bathroom. As you walk into the bathroom, bounce on the floor near the toilet. If it's "squishy," watch out. You may have to replace the flooring. Pull up any carpet or rug (without detaching it). Do you see evidence of water leakage, like curling or loose tiles? Think time and money. Look at the tile or tub enclosure. See evidence of water leaks? Press on the tub enclosure. If the area behind it is again "squishy," you're looking at hundreds of dollars to replace the enclosure, the wall, and possibly the tub or shower. The utility room is another area where you may see evidence of leakage or water damage. If there's a basement in the home, walk through and

Real Life

I was showing a home in a very good area to a young couple with two small children. This home had lots of possibilities, but had been rented for a long time. It obviously needed many repairs. As we walked through the hallway in the basement, I looked up and saw water stains on the ceiling. The more of the house we saw, the more trepidation I felt. The buyers asked me if I thought they should buy that home. I told them "no," because there was so much work that needed to be done, and I was afraid they would find much more work after they moved in (this was before the era of inspections, too). Well, they bought the home, did the work, got transferred two years later, and made a few thousand dollars! Taught me another lesson. To each his own. I felt like I had done my job, though, in cautioning them about buying a home with so many unknowns. If I'd been afraid of losing a commission, I may not have felt I could tell them my opinion. You should have the kind of agent who's not afraid to tell you *not* to purchase a home.

sniff. Does it smell "mildewy"? Could be a hidden basement leak. Glance up at the ceiling. See any water damage? Look for evidence of sloppy or faulty electrical wiring. Loose wires mean trouble.

I'm enclosing an inspection checklist in Figure 8.2. This checklist will guide you through the specifics of interior and exterior inspection. For dozens of tips on what to look for as you inspect a home, read the book from which this excellent checklist is printed: Robert Irwin's *The Home Inspection Troubleshooter* (Chicago: Dearborn Financial Publishing, Inc., 1995).

As you walk through the home, realize that all resale homes have things that need to be fixed. Your objective in walking through now is to get a sense of how much needs to be fixed and whether you want to take on such a project.

FIGURE 8.2 • One-Hour Inspection Checklist

CAUTION—NEVER DO ANYTHING THAT COULD HARM THE PROPERTY. ALWAYS ASK PERMISSION OF THE OWNER BEFORE TURNING ON OR OFF ANYTHING OR ATTEMPTING TO POKE AT, PICK UP, OR MOVE ITEMS.

Outside the Home

You should begin your inspection on the outside. Walk around the home and look for the following:

Drainage

- ❏ Any signs of mold and wood rot?
- ❏ Any standing puddles or damp earth?
- ❏ Any places where drainage from back to front of lot is obstructed?

Foundation

- ❏ Any cracks?
- ❏ Any other damage?
- ❏ Any water stains indicating earlier problems?
- ❏ Bulges?
- ❏ Leaning or settling?

If any of these are present, you may want to have a professional check it out to see whether the problem is minor or serious.

Electrical Service

- ❏ Is the cover in place on the main circuit breaker box?
- ❏ Are there any signs of sparking or fire on the outside?

House Walls

- ❏ Is all exposed wood painted or stained?
- ❏ Are all other surfaces painted?
- ❏ Any rotting wood?
- ❏ Any chipping, peeling, blistering, chalking paint?
- ❏ Any cracks?

The vast majority of cracks are minor, however, be careful they don't conceal any major structural cracking.

FIGURE 8.2 • One-Hour Inspection Checklist *(Continued)*

Metal Siding

- ❏ Any dents or scratches?
- ❏ Any bare metal showing?
- ❏ Are some pieces poorly joined?
- ❏ Are rusted nail heads showing?

Sometimes siding can be repaired and painted, but often the result is not very good looking or does not last very long.

Brick Walls

- ❏ Are the bricks properly sealed against moisture?
- ❏ Are there any cracked or missing bricks?
- ❏ If painted, is the paint cracked, chipped, or peeling?

If there are small problems, you may be able to handle them yourself. However, masonry repair can be heavy work and you may want to use a professional.

Stucco

- ❏ Cracks?
- ❏ Chipped, peeling, chalky paint?

Stucco can be painted, although those who put it on generally do not recommend this. Painting stucco often puts a finish on it that will last for many years, depending on the quality of the paint.

Well

- ❏ Does the seller have documentation showing water quality, pressure, and so on. Is it in good working order?

Pool and Spa

- ❏ Operation okay?
- ❏ Algae? Is water green, yellow, brown, or black?
- ❏ Any faulty equipment?
- ❏ Any Cracks Or Leaks?

Particularly pay attention to the clarity of the water and the walls and bottom. Also, be sure the equipment is working.

Septic Tank

- ❏ Any odors or overflows?
- ❏ Need cleaning (usually every five years)?
- ❏ Leach field okay? What about pump for below-grade tanks?

FIGURE 8.2 • One-Hour Inspection Checklist *(Continued)*

Roof

❏ Any wood shingles falling off?
❏ Tar paper showing through the shingles?
❏ Evidence of leaking?
❏ Any asphalt shingles decaying or breaking?
❏ Any asphalt shingles? Curling at edges?
❏ Areas of no gravel (on tar and gravel roof)?
❏ Any bubbling, curling, or crumbling (on tar & gravel roof)?
❏ Cracked tiles on tile roof?
❏ Punctures and tears on metal roof?
❏ Discoloration, peeling paint, or rust on metal roof?
❏ Leaks, rust, or cracks on flashing or gutters?
❏ Gutter separation from the house?

Inside the House

Walls and Flooring

❏ Scratches and marks on inside walls?
❏ Cracks on inside walls?
❏ Squeaks on floor?
❏ Uneven Floors?
❏ Broken, scratched, or loose floor tiles?
❏ Rotten or soiled carpeting?

Safety Features

❏ Fire extinguishers?
❏ Smoke alarms?
❏ Locks functional?
❏ Security system functional?

Slabs

❏ Cracks in cement slab?
❏ Tilting or settling of slab?
❏ Separation of slab from the peripheral foundation?

Electrical

❏ Ground wire connected at all plugs, switches, and outlets?
❏ Polarity of plugs okay?
❏ GFI circuitry in all wet areas?
❏ Wiring in good condition?

The above usually require the services of an electrician to check out.

FIGURE 8.2 • One-Hour Inspection Checklist *(Continued)*

Wood Burning Stove

❏ Are there any cracks, broken fire bricks, broken glass, loose or missing door insulator?
❏ Is the flue clean?
❏ Is the federal approval sticker in place?

Fireplace

❏ Does the damper work?
❏ Does it draw? Does it smoke?
❏ Does it have a spark arrestor?
❏ Are there any cracked bricks outside/inside?
❏ Are there water leaks where it goes through the ceiling?
❏ Is the mantel sagging? (check underneath)

Be aware that cracks in a fireplace are a serious problem as they may allow heat and flame to reach other areas of the structure. This should be checked out by a professional.

Bathrooms

❏ Are any faucets leaking?
❏ Any rusting or other pipe problems?
❏ Is there overly low/high water pressure?

Low water pressure indicates a more serious problem which may require replumbing the house. Too high water pressure may mean you need to have a water pressure regulator installed, usually not expensive but may require a plumber.

Toilets

❏ Does the mechanism work?
❏ Any leaks?
❏ Poor drainage (takes a long time to drain)?

The most common problem with toilets is that they run without shutting off. It's usually easy to fix this.

Tubs/Showers

❏ Leaks?
❏ Scratches and cracks?

FIGURE 8.2 • **One-Hour Inspection Checklist** *(Continued)*

Kitchen

- ❏ Does garbage disposal operate?
- ❏ Any leaks?
- ❏ Does dishwasher operate?
- ❏ Does it leak?
- ❏ Is it rusting?
- ❏ Is the overflow (located on the sink) clear?

Attic

- ❏ Is sunlight obvious when looking up through holes visible from the attic, indicating a roof problem?
- ❏ Are any old leaks visible?
- ❏ Are the pipes in good condition?
- ❏ Are the vents in good condition?
- ❏ Any insulation? How much? What kind?

Pedestals in the Basement or under the Home

- ❏ Has the dirt eroded from under the pad?
- ❏ Is the pad tilted, cracked, or otherwise damaged?
- ❏ Has the column lifted off the pad (or lifted the pad itself off the ground)?

Wiring

- ❏ What type is it?
- ❏ Is it adequate for the home?
- ❏ What is its condition?

Telephone and Cable Wiring

- ❏ Is it well grounded?
- ❏ Is it properly located?

Forced-Air Heating

- ❏ Are the ducts located at floor level or near the ceiling (floor best for heat, ceiling best for cooling)?
- ❏ Is the ductwork in good condition?
- ❏ Is the fan motor clean, without squeaks and working?
- ❏ Are there holes in the heat exchanger?

Electric Heating

- ❏ Is it adequate for the home?
- ❏ Any burned wiring?

FIGURE 8.2 • **One-Hour Inspection Checklist** *(Continued)*

Circulating Water-Heating System

- ❑ Any leaks?
- ❑ Is the pump, motor, or valves worn?
- ❑ Is the heater worn?

Oil Furnace

- ❑ Is there adequate storage (500-gallon tank or more)?
- ❑ Any oil leaks?
- ❑ Any water corrosion?

Hot Water Heater

- ❑ What is its age and size? Is it adequate?
- ❑ Any leaks?
- ❑ Any deposits?
- ❑ Is the safety pressure valve operational?
- ❑ Is it vented property?
- ❑ Is it tied down (in case of an earthquake)?

Insulation

- ❑ Is the home insulated? Ceiling? Walls? Floor?
- ❑ Is the R-rating of the insulation adequate for the home?
- ❑ Are the windows and doors insulated?

Earthquake Retrofitting

- ❑ Is there diagonal bracing throughout the home?
- ❑ Is the stud spacing no more than 16 inches on center?
- ❑ Is the foundation tied down?
- ❑ Is the steel roof tied down?

Keep your comments to yourself (and your agent). I've said this before, but it bears repeating: Don't tell anyone except your buyer's agent your impressions of a home. Remind your buyer's agent, too, not to disclose any information to other agents that could hurt your negotiating position. Let me tell you how an innocent comment can cost you thousands of dollars in negotiating power. Let's say you've been looking for homes for a few weeks. Your agent has left his business card in each home he's shown you. The listing agent picks up the real estate business cards left in the home. Then, he calls each of the agents who left cards to ask them what their buyers thought of the home. He asks if the buyers thought the home was priced right, and if the agent thought the home was priced right. Armed with this information, the listing agent uses these comments to get the seller to reduce the price or fix up the home. He also uses the information to help the seller strategize negotiating tactics on offers.

When all agents represented the seller, they had an obligation to tell the listing agent theirs and their buyers' opinions about the home pricing. However, when agents represent buyers, they have no obligation to give the listing agent this kind of feedback. In fact, it's not good for the buyer's negotiating position if the buyer's agent says to the listing agent, "Yes, we thought the home was priced well." This is communicated to the seller, and sets up expectations in his mind. The next day, the buyer decides to make an offer, and offers 20 percent below asking price. The seller, having heard the feedback from the listing agent, is aghast and insulted. So, if you have a buyer's agent, instruct her not to give the listing agent feedback about what you thought about the home.

The Decision: Have You Found the Right Property for You?

You've been inspecting properties for the past three weeks. You've found a property that you think fits your needs. So, you go ahead and make a decision—at least, you think now you'll just jump right in and make an offer. However, from working with many buyers, I know that may not be what happens. Here are two very creative ways buyers put off buying the home they say they really want to buy.

Deciding not to decide.   As you look for homes, you think how wonderful it will be to finally find one and make that buying decision. You think it will be wonderful, until it happens. Then, you'll be frightened, because the day of decision is here now. Many times, buyers become so frightened to make a decision, that they use creative means to decide not to decide. This is what happens: The buyer falls in love with the home, and just can't decide to make an offer. So, he says to the agent, "It will be there if it's meant to be." Making a statement like that takes the decision out of your own hands. After all, you can't expect other buyers interested in that property to be psychic enough to hold back their offers so it's "meant to be" for you!

Deciding not to decide puts your agent in a quandary. Let's say your agent really feels that a particular home is the home for you. When you throw the "if it's meant to be" phrase out, you frustrate your agent. He knows that particular home is the best buy for you financially, and that it really fits your needs. What can the agent do to let you know you're missing the best opportunity he thinks you'll find? He doesn't want to use the old "it will be gone tomorrow" routine, even though he thinks it probably will be gone tomorrow. He doesn't want you to feel pressured. However, if you don't buy this home, the agent knows he will not be able to find another anywhere near the qualifications of this one for you.

Here's what to do if you're stuck in indecision: Sit down with your agent so you can recap the state of the market. Is it a "fast" market? Are several offers coming in at once? Take a look at the number of real estate agents' business cards in the home. If you can see a pattern of previewing or showings for that home, you know it's popular. If you see the same agent's card there two or three times, chances are there's another person just like you who's just as interested, and making a final decision. As my agent advisers remind me, you must think of other buyers as *your adversaries* at this point.

After having recapped the market, have your agent call the listing agent and ask about the number of showings per week and offers on that home. If there are several showings per week, it's a popular home. Realize, finally, that you and the agent have absolutely no idea when someone else will make a buying decision. We know that some behavioral styles make them fast, and some take lots of time. You just hope now that your competition for this home is an analyzer!

Insider Secret

☞ Your agent can't stop someone else from making an offer.

Another way buyers decide on indecision.

Buyers have another way to put off making a buying decision. They direct their agent to "call the listing agent and tell him to call you if an offer comes in, so we can decide if we want to make an offer. Tell him not to let the seller sign another offer until we have a chance to make an offer, too." By directing their agent to verbally spar with the seller, they've conveniently avoided committing themselves on paper. Your agent dutifully calls the listing agent. The next day, that listing agent has not one offer but *three* offers on the property of your choice. The listing agent has other things on his mind now besides calling your agent, and he doesn't have to drum up other offers when he's got three fine ones—bona fide offers in writing. The next day, though, your agent calls you to tell you the home has been sold. Who are you mad at? Your agent. Remember, the listing agent has no obligation to give any courtesies to a buyer who hasn't put his offer in writing. In fact, he has an obligation only to the seller, to present all offers that are in writing.

Getting Ready to Make Your Offer

If you have a buyer's agent, your agent should prepare a market analysis showing the relative value of the property. This written analysis is the same type of analysis listing agents use to price a property, which I discussed in Chapter 7. The analysis should include homes sold and closed, homes on the market, and homes whose listings have expired. Expect your agent to go over each point with you, and explain the relative value the comparable sales, or "comps," show. If possible, drive past some of the homes your agent has described in the market analysis.

Don't Ask If the Seller Will Take Your Offer

While my husband Dick was in real estate, he had lots of singular adventures (that is, he thought what happened to him only happened to him!). In truth, Dick's experiences are relived with agents and buyers often; his experiences, and especially as this DJ promoter entertainingly tells them, provide me with material in my books! Dick was working with a nice young couple, and found them a new home they loved. The price was $123,500. They asked Dick to call the builder and see if he'd take $121,000. The builder said, yes, and, of course, expected to see an offer at that price. Dick hung up the phone, turned to the buyers and told them the builder had agreed to their offer. They looked at each other and said, "Okay. We'll write it lower." So, Dick had to take an offer of $120,000 to a builder who was expecting $121,000. Needless to say, the builder was really upset with Dick. Of course, Dick was upset with the buyers, and the buyers, although they got the home—for $121,000, didn't have a spectacular relationship with the builder either! Don't ask your agent to ask the seller what he'll take so you can offer something lower. The seller doesn't need to keep his verbal promise, either, to sell to you at a certain price. Until each party puts pen to paper and signs that there is mutual agreement on all the terms in the offer, there is no binding contract.

The Properties Are Located, the View Focused

In this chapter, I've helped you inspect properties, and narrow the field to a home you want to buy. Now, you're ready to create your negotiating strategies to make sure you get the property you want, at a price you can afford.

Frequently Asked Questions

Q. My agent has been making a list of homes for me to see and sending me to inspect them on weekends when other agents are holding homes open. Should my agent be touring these homes with me?

A. Generally, yes. It's important your agent (especially if he's a buyer's agent), is with you, giving you information about areas, condition, and relative pricing. The only time an agent should give you an address of a property to see is when the agent is not able to be with you; it may be a very hot market, and you might miss seeing the property if you don't see it now.

Q. My wife and I have looked at 56 properties. We don't like any of them. We feel the agent just isn't showing us what we want to see. What should we do?

A. First, revisit the Home Information Form with your agent. Have your priorities changed? Point out, on the form, the differences between what you described you wanted in a property and what the agent is showing you. Ask the agent why what you're seeing is different from what you said you wanted to see.

Q. Our agent insists on showing us homes in an uncomfortably high price range. How can we see homes in the price range we want?

A. Tell your agent your concerns *directly*. Ask for a tour in your desired price range. Maybe what's going on is that you are describing a property that the agent feels is available only in the higher price range. You'll know the right price range for you when you look at that lower price range and compare what you get in each range.

9

Advocate or Adversary?

How to Partner a Negotiating Strategy to Work in Your Favor

You've found it—the home you want to buy. In this chapter, I'll give you information on how to handle this stage of the buying process, including:

- Strategies to create an effective negotiating approach
- Tips on how your agent can assist you in the development of these strategies
- Guidelines on what to put in your offer

Please note: In most states, agents draft purchase and sale agreements. However, in a few states, attorneys write these contracts. Check the procedure in your state.

An Overview of the Offering Process

You'll be strategizing with your agent to create an "offer to purchase." This is a written contract between you and the seller. It's created on a preprinted form with many blanks to fill in. Your agent should have provided you a copy of the type of agreement used in your area during the consultation period, so you can review the form. In addition to your filling in the blanks on the form, you may write other clauses, conditions of your purchase. The agreement spells out exactly how you want to purchase the property.

After You've Signed the Offer

It's easy to become confused when you start negotiating with the seller, because the paperwork starts flying fast. Certain protocol must be observed to make sure the outcome is a mutual agreement with all required signatures. Here's a description of that protocol. First, your agent will give you a copy of the agreement you just completed. (You should receive a copy of the agreement each time you sign or make changes to it, so you have a record of the negotiations and of the changes and agreements you and the seller made).

Next, your agent makes an appointment to present the offer to the seller. The seller reviews your offer, and can do the following:

- Reject your offer and return it, without signing it, to your agent. (That means the seller didn't even want to let you know the terms he would take; it's up to you to make another new offer or forget buying the property.)
- Sign your offer as you presented it.
- Make a counteroffer.

A counteroffer is a seller's answer to your offer, and the most common type of answer buyers get from sellers. A counteroffer means the seller doesn't accept what you offer, but is willing to tell you, in writing, what he will accept for his property. In a counteroffer, the seller makes changes on the offer to fit his needs. That way, he's letting you know the terms he will accept. Some common areas sellers counteroffer on are the price, some of the financing terms, or the closing date, for instance. Depending on the custom in your area, a counteroffer can be made by a change written directly on the offer. The change is initialed by the seller, who then gets a copy of the agreement. In other areas, the counteroffer may be created by writing it on another form, named an "addendum" or "counteroffer addendum."

When you receive the seller's counteroffer the ball is back in your court. You can reject the counteroffer and move on to another property. You can accept the counteroffer and buy the home. Or, you too can counteroffer. How long can the counteroffer process go on? Sometimes for days, even weeks. Usually there are two or three counteroffers, then final agreement.

Back to the three choices the seller has initially in dealing with your offer. If the offer has been accepted by the seller just as you wrote it, your agent will bring back the seller-signed offer for your final signature. You will be given a copy of the completed contract. You've bought a home!

If the offer has been rejected flatly by the seller, you have two choices. You can change your offer and present it again, or go on to the next property.

It is important to remember that you get a copy of each agreement you sign. Each time you make a change in an offer, be sure to initial and date the change. Check, too, to be sure the seller has initialed and dated all changes on the offer. You want to create a paper trail of the transaction negotiation.

Services Your Agent Should Provide Now

During the time you're making an offer (or offers), on a property, what an agent can do for you somewhat depends on her agency relationship to you. I'm going to describe what a buyer's agent should do for you, because that's the highest level of representation you can receive—legally. As mentioned in Chapter 4, a buyer's agent can provide some services that a seller's agent or dual agent legally isn't supposed to provide. Buyer's agent services at this point include the following:

- Preparing a market analysis on the home you want to purchase
- Telling you the offers that have been previous made on the subject home (if your agent can get the particulars)
- Advising you on negotiating strategies, including a first offering price (Agents with other agency relationships with you such as a seller's agent or dual agent can't give you advice on any offering price except full price.)
- Showing you other properties during the time you're negotiating on this one (so you can be ready to make an offer on another property in case this one doesn't work out)

Review these services with your agent to be sure you'll be getting these services now.

At this stage of the game, you want an assertive agent. When buyers start the buying process, they are concerned that they have plenty of time to make a buying decision. So, some buyers choose an agent they think will be really easygoing. They want to avoid the "pushy" agent, the agent who will show them too few homes and force a decision. Or, they choose a new agent because they can direct the new agent and stay in control of their buying situation. At first, the buyers really like this kind of agent, because they feel comfortable. They know they're really in control of the buying situation. However, buyers can start feeling uncomfortable when they want some guidance and direction as they try to narrow the field and choose a home. The "wimp" or "wimpette" agent I've described will not help the buyer narrow the field. He or she won't go to bat for a buyer during this offer and counteroffering process. After all this agent doesn't want to be "pushy." If you feel your agent is receding into the woodwork when it comes time to make a decision, you should tell your agent your expectations. Now, you need an agent who will help you plan your strategy and then sell your position to the seller.

Insider Secret

☛ That laid-back agent who you chose because he wasn't "pushy" may be your worst choice now.

Market Conditions Affect Your Offer

Earlier, I mentioned making your agent your partner in the buying process. Then he is your advocate, not your adversary. This is an important relationship to maintain now, because you must have his expertise to figure out what you want to offer. Appraising market conditions is an important consideration in deciding on your offer, and one where your agent adds invaluable expertise.

Review Buying Conditions in Your Area

During your consultation with your agent, he should have educated you about real estate trends in your area. As you viewed homes, you saw evidence of these trends. Now, it's time to get an update on what's happening. Your agent will complete the form in Figure 9.1 as a guide you can use in preparing your overall buying strategy. The trends of the market in your area will greatly impact how you design your negotiating strategy.

FIGURE 9.1 • Planning Your Buying Process: How the Market Affects Your Buying Decisions

Part of your planning process includes being aware of market conditions in your area. I'll research the market to give you the latest statistics on market trends, so you can make a smart buying decision.

Number of homes on the market in your price range/market area ____

Number of homes in your price range sold in last 30 days _____

Number of days on the market for these homes _____

Percent of sales price to list price _____

Buyer competition for homes in your price range is: High_____ Medium____ Low____

Market trends _____

Your buying/negotiating strategies for this market _____

_____

_____

_____

_____

_____

_____

_____

_____

_____

_____

_____

_____

_____

One Type of Market: Slow as Molasses

If there are many homes for sale and few buyers, the market is called a "buyers' market." That means buyers are in the driver's seat. There aren't going to be multiple offers on one property, because there are so many properties to choose from. In fact, properties in this kind of market may stay on the market a long time. Commonly, sellers must reduce their prices to attract buyers. Does this mean, then, that your buying strategy should be to make a low offer? Not necessarily. It depends on the property. You'll want to check how many days the property has been on the market. Ask your agent to do a study to tell you the number of days, on average, homes stay on the market for this price range and area. That will give you the best indicator of the strength of the market in that particular price range. Even in a very slow market, the best properties can sell within a few days. It only takes one buyer.

The Opposite Market: Fast as a Raging River

In a seller's market, there are few homes for sale, and these are selling fast. There are many buyers vying for a home. It's just supply and demand at work. Homes are on the market for a few days only, and there are commonly multiple offers. Sellers obviously do not have to accept low offers or give many concessions to buyers. Offers at less than full price just aren't accepted.

How do you know that you're buying in a "seller's market"? Have your agent do a study of how many days houses are on the market for your price range and area. If you see that homes are staying on the market only a few days, be prepared to act fast. Your agent can tell you if there are multiple offers on properties, and how those offers are structured. Be prepared that you will be in competition with another buyer (or more).

The Picture in Your Local Area

Looking at the big picture on the national and local scene is important, but it's also important to assess what's happening in the price range and area where you want to buy. That price range of home may be experiencing a different market trend from the overall market. For instance, let's say that you read the market is sluggish in the Northwest, where you're being transferred. You're excited to think when you buy a home, you'll be able to make a killing. You drive around the area and see many signs, especially on the larger homes and nicer areas. Newspaper advertising is full of homes for sale.

Insider Secret

☛ Overall trends don't mean as much as what's happening on your street.

You have some special considerations as a buyer. You're a first-time homebuyer, and you're buying a home with a low down payment. Since this is your first home, you're buying in the lowest price range the area has. You also want to buy in a newer area, where you believe homes will appreciate, and appear to be in good condition.

Now, when you start looking for your home with your agent, you find that there are lots of "sold" signs on the homes. Your agent tells you that the homes in your price range are selling fast. But, you just read that home sales in the Northwest are sluggish. Who's right? Although the general picture in the Northwest is that of a buyer's market, with plenty of homes available, it's different in your price range. There are too many higher-priced homes in the Northwest for the number of buyers. So, market time for these homes is many months. In contrast, there are too few homes in your price range and desired area. Market time is short and demand is high. If you design your negotiating strategy with the idea that the market is sluggish, you probably won't get the home you want. So, pay attention not only to the overall picture, but what's going on in the price range and area you want. Your agent can help you differentiate between general area trends and trends in your buying range and area.

Putting Together Your Negotiating Strategy

When it comes to making offers, there are other considerations besides market conditions. In this section, I'll give you advice about a few of them.

Dealing with the Seller Strategy of Overpricing

No matter the type of market, some sellers like to list their homes at a high price—to start. Sellers are always afraid that they will leave some money on the table. So, they seldom want to list their home at the price their agent suggests. Some sellers believe the agent will give them a low price, just to get a fast sale. Some sellers believe that buyers will make low offers, no matter how the home is priced. Checking the history of the listing will give you valuable negotiating insights. Have your agent check to see if the seller has reduced his price, and how many times he's reduced it, plus the amount of those price reductions. In general, the longer the home has been on the market, and the more price reductions, the "softer" the price usually is. That is, if you're looking for a property you can buy for much less than the seller is asking, look for a seller who's listed his home too high, and has reduced the price several times. By the way, recent survey results from the NAR showed that homes that stay on the market a long time sell for at least 10 percent less than homes that sell fast.

As a practical matter, agents know that when a property's price has been reduced several times over a period of several months, offers get wild and loose. Why? Because no one knows what the seller's real bottom line is—or should be. The good news for you when you see a property like this is that any offer will probably be considered, because the seller is acting like a desperate marketer. The bad news for you is that it's difficult to determine real value. The best thing for you to do in this kind of situation is to have your agent do a market analysis and give you advice on the kind of relative value of that property.

For Those of You Who Believe You Should Never Pay Full Price

Have you ever seen someone pay too much for something—or at least, you thought they paid too much—only to find that it proved to be an astute investment? I worked for several years for an owner of a large real estate company, who told me when he bought the company, which then consisted of two offices, everyone told him he paid too much. At the time, maybe he did. However, the prior owner accepted his low down payment and easy terms. That's the only way he could buy the property. In ten years, my employer built that company into a multimillion dollar concern. Did he pay too much?

What if he had walked away from the transaction, because his principle was never to pay full price? I've seen people buy properties at over full price that turned out to be astute investments. I've seen people pay what they considered bargain prices for properties that turned out to be no bargain. When you're deciding on a negotiating strategy, don't let old buying principles rule your decisions. Treat each situation on its own merits.

You're Buying Future Value

Sometimes, buyers get too caught up in getting a home that's a "real deal" (whatever that is). When I first started selling real estate, I, too, thought my job was to get the home for a buyer at thousands off the list price. What I found, though, was that was the wrong game. Why? What someone pays for a home may not have much to do with how much money they make on it when they sell. First, selling a home in less than three years means that, to make a profit, you'll have to be able to sell the home for more than all those improvements cost you—drapes, landscaping, etc. It means you'll have to recover your closing costs, both as a buyer and as a seller. So, short term, your costs and what happens to the market pretty much determine how much money you'll make—if any.

Let's look at the situation a little longer-term. Let's say you bought your home seven years ago. At that time, you paid top dollar, for it was a very competitive market. You thought you might be paying too much, but you had no choice. Now, it's seven years later, and you're being transferred to Cleveland. You find out your home is worth $40,000 more than you paid for it. You're making more money than your friends told you that you would. Why? When we buy real state, we're buying *future value*. You and I don't know how a neighborhood will develop, or how the rest of the area will be affected economically. We don't know what buyers will do for—or to—their homes. Will the "improvements" you make add to the value, or redirect it?

There are many variables that determine future value. To agonize over a few thousand dollars to get the home you really want will seem, when you look back on it, like a trivial matter. After you've struggled through the first few months with your new home (and house payment), bought all those things you must have to make that house your home, made improvements, etc., your life starts to settle down, and you can see your decision from a different prospective.

In my experience, the biggest homebuyer losers were those who decided not to buy that year, or not to buy a home because they couldn't get a seller to reduce his price another $1,000. Remember, once a seller gets the closing check in hand, he never gets another dime from that property. Once a home is yours, you've got control, and the potential for appreciation is all yours.

Structure a Win-Win Negotiation

Do you like to win at any cost? Do you want to feel as though you got the buy of the century—at any expense to the seller? Or, do you want to create a win-win situation (where both you and the seller feel it's a good agreement)? I have worked with buyers who thought they had to win big, making the seller lose big, to feel okay about their purchase. These are buyers who direct the agent to write a very low offer on an attractive property, a property that's just been listed. They also direct an agent to include several "weasel" clauses, wordings to let them get out of the offer easily. Every part of the offer is structured so they win and the seller loses.

Here's why that approach is a bad idea. When I, the agent, go to present the offer, I want the seller to think he's winning something, so he'll give you what you want. A guiding principle of negotiation is, to get what you want, you must give the other party what he wants. However, when no part of the offer is beneficial to the seller, it's very difficult to get a seller to sign that offer. Remember, too, that a listing agent is sitting with the seller, explaining, from his perspective, whether the offer is beneficial to the seller.

I can hear you now. You're arguing that any offer is better for the seller than none. You'll try to tell me to convince the seller to sign this horribly awful offer—because, if he signs, his house is sold. From my experience, if the offer is really awful, that ploy just doesn't work. Some offers are so pitiful and disrespectful to sellers it's difficult to get the seller to respond even with a counteroffer. Sellers can feel so affronted that they refuse to give any hints as to what they'll take for the property. Al Johnson, on my agent advisory panel, advises buyers not to attempt to "vanquish" the seller! If you do, you'll get a much higher counteroffer than you would have gotten had your offer been better— if you get a counteroffer at all.

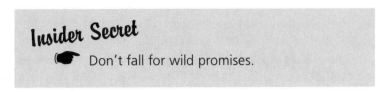

Insider Secret
☛ Don't fall for wild promises.

Agents Can't Get Sellers to Sign Poor Offers

When it gets to the point of creating an offer, some agents go over-board in making promises to buyers. If an agent promises he can absolutely get the home you want at the price and terms you want to pay, watch out. No agent can make a seller sign an offer. If you think your agent is making promises he can't follow through on, tell him directly. Otherwise, he may fib to the seller, or fib to you about what happened in that offer presentation. At this point, you need complete trust, honesty, and openness with your agent. If you feel you're not getting it, and talking to the agent doesn't help, call his broker and discuss the situation.

Creating Your Offer to Purchase

As you work with your agent, you'll start to get a sense of the type of market you're in. You'll zero in on your price range and area, and create your overall negotiating strategy based on market trends. Now, let's look at creating the offer. I'll give you some guidelines about several considerations in your offer. But, I caution you to rely on your agent for the practices and legalities of your area.

Deciding on the Price You Should Offer

First, get some statistics from your agent about the relationship of sales price to list price in that area, so you'll have a frame of reference. A recent NAR survey shows that buyers, on average, negotiated $3,500 off a purchase price of $120,000. In the Northwest, the ratio of sales price to list price is 97 percent of last list price. That means, on a home listed for $200,000, the final agreement was at $194,000. Notice I said

-20% Real Life

Jim and Jan were making a real change in their lives. They were finally empty nesters and were going to relocate from their conventional three-bedroom rambler to a more "adventurous" type of home. They really wanted a view, too. We started looking at homes together, and, at one point, viewed a multilevel new home with a view. Since the home was only being framed, Jim and Jan didn't feel they could really see what it would look like, and decided not to make an offer. We looked at many other homes, and couldn't find what they wanted.

One Sunday, they drove by the new home, and there was an open house sign. They went in and chatted with the listing agent, who was holding the home open. She suggested that the builder would take an offer—an offer 20 percent below list price! (Note: As a listing agent, she shouldn't have said anything of the sort, unless the seller had directed her to do so.) The thought that they could buy this home for 20 percent under list price excited Jim and Jan. They didn't want to buy the home, though, from the listing agent, and so they called me. They told me that the listing agent had told them the seller would take an offer 20 percent below list price, and directed me to write such an offer. I had worked with builders for years, and I knew that 20 percent below list price meant that the builder would be reaching into his pocket to close! At the time, builders in the area were generally not accepting any offers below list price. I explained all this to Jim and Jan, but they turned deaf ears. After all, the *listing* agent had given them the inside scoop. Who was I to tell them differently?

Jim, Jan, and I met, and wrote the offer. I asked Jim and Jan to help me with the negotiating strategy, because I couldn't think of a good rationale to use with the builders to explain this offer. Was that all they thought the property was worth? "No," they said. Was that all they could afford? "No."

So, what is it? How can I convince a builder that it's in his best interests to reach into his pocket to sell this home to these buyers? They had no answer, except to direct me to tell the builder that the listing agent had suggested the offer. Boy, I knew that would go over big!

I called the builder and arranged to meet at the builder's office late that afternoon. When I walked in, I found three expectant faces staring at me, all building partners. Now, builders are very straightforward. This is their business. They don't want the small talk and the "they just love your home" jabber. They don't want the agent to explain the offer. They just want to see the offer and figure out their bottom line. So, I gave them the offer. Two of three of the partners were so angry they refused to read past the price, and got up to leave. The other partner looked like he wanted to hit me. This was really going well. At this rate, I wouldn't even get the builders to write down what they would accept.

Finally, I told them how the buyers got the idea for the price (from their listing agent). Of course, this didn't make a lot of points, either, but I had no other options. I explained to the builders, if they would counteroffer, in writing of course, I could tell their story to the buyers. So, they did, giving me a counteroffer of full price. (It's that reaction to being vanquished.) I'm convinced, if I hadn't gotten the builders to answer the offer in writing, the buyers never would have believed that the builders had a different price in mind than 20 percent off list price. The buyers would have thought I just didn't do a good job presenting their offer.

This story has a happy ending. Jim and Jan bought the home for close to full price, moved in, and are enjoying a new adventure—with a stunning view. However, a short-sighted listing agent almost ruined a sale. Lucky for Jim and Jan that they had a tenacious agent like me, who was willing to hang in there, take the abuse from the builders, and get the real story to present back to the buyers.

last list price. That means that the home could have been reduced in price several times. When it finally got to the price that buyers thought was reasonable, buyers made offers.

Americans generally don't negotiate much. When we go to Nordstrom to buy a pair of shoes, we don't offer to pay $10 less than the sticker price. (Of course, I gave that analogy to a buyer once, and he informed me that he always negotiated on shoes at Nordstrom. I was so shocked I forgot to ask if it worked!) I think our repugnance at negotiating is a reason that the Saturn automobile has been so popular. The sticker price is the price. When you buy a Saturn, you don't have to wonder if someone got a better deal than you did. You also don't have to go through the hassles of the negotiation process.

New home offers. In most areas of the United States, in good markets, new homes are sold like Saturns. The sticker price is the price. The builder usually wants to retain the integrity of the sticker price, so, instead of giving you a reduction off the list price, she may throw in a fence or garage door opener (if she throws in anything). Your agent can fill you in on the idiosyncrasies of the area.

Resale home offers. Unfortunately, resale homes aren't sold like Saturns. I say "unfortunately," because, when homes sell for less than list price, it means you and your agent must do plenty of research and strategizing to determine a good first offer. I'm giving you percentage of sale price to list price, so you have some frame of reference. Just note: A reduction of $6,000 isn't a lot of money off the list price of the $200,000 home. Now, if that $200,000 home is in poor condition, has been on the market a long time, has had earlier price reductions, chances are the seller will take a lower offer. Just remember my story about Jim and Jan: Don't make that offer so ridiculous that the seller refuses to consider your offer. You need to retain the goodwill of the seller to get the best price.

Worksheet for creating an offer. Since there are several variables to consider when deciding on your offer, I've created the worksheet in Figure 9.2 to help you through the process.

Your Deposit

Typically, purchase and sale agreements (offers) require a monetary deposit. This can be in the form of a promissory note or a check. Which puts you in a more favorable negotiating position? A check, of course. How large a check? From your negotiating position, large enough so that the seller thinks you are "in earnest." (In some areas, purchase and sale agreements are called "earnest money agreements." The deposit is called "earnest money.") Don't be clever and give your agent a note for $25, or a measly check for $200. Think what that says about your negotiating position. You want your agent to be able to say to the seller, "This buyer really wants to buy your home. He has deposited $5,000 to show he's in earnest." I found that a reasonably large deposit (there are limits about what is "reasonable") was one of the best negotiating tools I could use on behalf of the buyer. It's hard for sellers to think in terms of getting sales proceeds of hundreds of thousands of dollars. Yet, they can identify with a check for $5,000.

What happens if the seller doesn't accept your offer? You get the money back. There are various practices around the country relating to promissory notes and checks. These are concerned with the deposit of, the time frame of, and the amounts. I won't go into those practices here, but your agent should explain the practices in that particular area.

Can you lose your deposit? Yes, if you violate the terms of the agreement. Again, ask your agent under what conditions you could forfeit your deposit. Be sure you understand how your deposit will be handled. Will your deposit be cashed? Yes. When? That depends on how the offer is written. Again, check with your agent. Many miscommunications occur about deposits. That again is where your competent agent becomes invaluable.

Contingencies in Your Offer

A contingency is a provision requiring that a certain condition be satisfied or an event occur in order for the contract to become binding. An example would be your contingency on financing. Most of the time, buyers don't pay cash for homes. Instead, they go to a bank or mortgage company and apply for a loan to supplement their down payment. Because you need to have a commitment from a lending institution to buy your home, you make your offer contingent on your ability to get financing, usually within 30 days. At the end of that time, if you can't

---

FIGURE 9.2 • **Worksheet for Creating an Offer**

Property_____ Listed price _____

Market Trends

Area market conditions: Seller's market_____ Buyer's market _____

Number of homes available in price range/area _____

Number of sales in this quarter _____

Days on market for this price range/area: _____

Percent of sales price to list price in this price range and area _____%

Buyers' offering habits for this price range/area _____

Subject Property Listing History

Number of days on market _____ Number of price reductions_____

Price reduction history _____ Listed with _____companies

Number of offers_____ Price of offers $_____

Evaluation of Property

Positive amenities to support value _____

_____

Property improvements needed (indicate a dollar figure):

Landscaping $_____ Exterior $_____ Walkways, driveway $_____

Roof $_____ Other improvements on exterior: $_____

Interior paint $_____ Repair $_____ Appliances $_____

Plumbing $_____ Heating $_____ Electrical $_____

Other improvements on interior $_____

Offer Strategy

First offering price $_____ Terms_____

Contingencies_____

_____

Benefits to seller of accepting this offer:

_____

_____

get financing, you may cancel your offer and get your deposit back. Generally, though, if you remove your contingency, and then refuse to close the transaction, you will lose your deposit. There's one contingency required by law when purchasing a home built before 1978. It is an addendum giving a buyer ten days to obtain a lead paint hazard risk assessment. Because homes built before that date commonly were painted with lead-based paint, which can be harmful to humans, this inspection is important for a buyer to have done.

Actually, disputes over who gets the deposit when one party defaults on the agreement to purchase can get very complicated. (More about that in the next chapter.) The important point here, though, is to discuss with your agent what specific contingencies you'll need in your offer, what's practiced in your area, how you'll remove those contingencies, reasonable time frame to satisfy the contingencies, and what happens if you don't remove those contingencies.

Home inspections.   Very few buyers buy a home today (even a new one) without putting a contingency in the offer that says their final agreement is contingent on their approval of a home inspection. The buyer chooses a home inspector, at his expense, and orders the inspection done. How will you find an inspector? Your agent can recommend three. Why three? To ensure that you pick the one you want. When agents recommend only one inspector, and a home defect is found after closing, buyers find it convenient to blame the agent. Many inspectors now are members of the American Society of Home Inspectors, and I recommend you employ an inspector who's a member. Anyone can call himself an inspector, and they range from very competent to not competent at all, for there are no tests or competencies required to call oneself an inspector.

When you're picking an inspector, be sure the inspector is really working for you. I worked in an area where the inspector slanted his reports so they were favorable to homes listed by a certain agency. I don't know whether that was because he wanted more business from the listing agency or he got a kickback from that agency. My advice is to pick a reputable inspector who will give you a reasonably detailed report.

Meet the inspector when he is scheduled to do the property inspection. Go through the property with the inspector, so you can get a "live" report about the problems areas on the property. Find out which are important problems, and which are not. Sometimes, reading an inspection report, the smallest problem may appear to be a real concern. Getting the inspector's verbal judgments is a good way to put his report in perspective.

Pay close attention to the wording in your offer concerning removing the inspection contingency. How soon? How is it removed? What happens if you find something you want the seller to fix? What happens if you decide, because of the inspection, you don't want to buy the property? These are all questions your agent can advise you about.

Time frames.   A competent agent will counsel you about the various time frames in an offer. How long will it take you to get financing? Should you be preapproved or prequalified prior to writing this offer? If you have a home to sell, what kind of contingencies and time frames are reasonable?

One of the most important time frames to discuss with your agent is how long you should give a seller to answer your offer. In your best interest, it's generally the same day. Why? You don't want to give the seller time to gather your offer and compare it with lots of others. That puts you in a bidding war. However, if you give the seller until midnight to answer your offer, and he doesn't answer you, you can still extend your offer by doing nothing. If you want to withdraw your offer, simply call your agent and instruct him to tell the seller the offer is withdrawn.

Signatures, counteroffers, and time frames can get pretty complicated, so you'll want to communicate clearly with your agent on how the process works. If your agent seems unsure about time frames, ask your agent to check with his broker.

All the time frames in your offer must coordinate with each other. For example, if you have a home to sell, you must coordinate that time frame with your time frame for closing. It's best to sketch these time frames in total on a calendar with your agent as you are preparing the offer, to be sure you don't have the cart before the horse. (I've seen some time frames in offers that were impossible to achieve, all because the agent didn't understand the time frames needed, or didn't use a calendar when charting all the time frames.)

Getting someone else's approval about your purchase.   Sometimes, buyers want someone else to approve the purchase of the home. You may decide you want your mom and dad to tell you it's a "good buy." If so, how do you want their approval? Do you want to take them through the home prior to your writing the offer? If they don't "anoint" your purchase, will you decide not to buy the home? These are important considerations for you to make. If you do want someone else's advice on your purchase, take them through the home prior to your writing your offer. This way, the offer doesn't get an additional contingency. Remember, the more contingencies, the weaker the offer to the seller.

Sometimes buyers put contingencies in offers, such as "Contingent on my parents approving this sale." Sellers know that there is no "deal," then, even if buyer and seller come to agreement on all the other terms on this offer, until the parents approve the sale. What are the parents approving? The purchase of the property, or the way the offer is written? Be careful about what you expect someone else to inspect and approve. If your parents aren't familiar with the wording of an offer, familiar with the practices of the area, and willing to be educated about the process as you have been, you can expect more work on your part—and not necessarily good advice.

Having attorneys review your offer.   Attorneys really want to move further into the world of real estate. Why? They feel there's lots of opportunity for making money. In the past few years, attorneys have become more involved in real estate, especially in closing transactions. It depends on the area as to how attorneys are involved. Find out from your agent how attorneys figure into the process of writing, reviewing, and closing real estate transactions in your area.

If you're in doubt about specific wording in your offer, or ramifications of this wording, have your attorney review your offer *prior* to presentation. A good agent, by the way, will suggest that you have a real estate attorney review your offer if there are areas where your agent believes you need legal advice. Be wary, though, of writing your offer first, and then having an attorney review it as a contingency. If you make the final acceptance of your offer contingent upon your attorney's review and approval, you have weakened your negotiating position with the seller.

A word of caution about attorneys: Like doctors, attorneys often specialize in certain kinds of law. An attorney specializing in divorce will not know the practices of the area regarding real estate. As you can tell from this book, there are many real estate practices that are specific to a particular area. Unless an attorney specializes in real estate, there's no way for him to know the niceties of the area. For instance, in Puget

Sound, it's common to give the seller a deposit of 3 to 5 percent of the purchase price in the form of a check. But, an attorney, writing an offer most attractive for a buyer, may suggest a promissory note for $100. The attorney thinks he's doing the right thing, acting as a buyer's advocate. However, to the listing agent and the seller, it looks as if it's just a tactic to prove the buyer is not very much "in earnest" about purchasing that property.

In a hot market where there are several offers at once on a home, all other parts of offers being equal, the offer with the largest deposit wins the home. If the attorney were a good real estate attorney, he would know that the buyer's offer should be competitive enough to attract the seller to answer the offer. If you want an attorney to review your paperwork, and you don't know a real estate attorney, ask for three referrals from your agent. Call each attorney, and choose the one you're most comfortable with.

You're Almost Home!

You've assessed the market trends with your agent. You've prepared an offer to present you, the buyer, in the best light to the seller. You've strategized with your agent about how to present the offer so the seller perceives he's also a winner. You've structured your offer to reflect the specific market, the condition of the property, and you've taken into consideration the amount of time the home has been on the market. Now, it's time to present and negotiate the offer.

Frequently Asked Questions

Q. My agent has shown me lots of homes. I've actually found a couple I'd like to buy. However, my agent seems in no hurry. What should I do to convince this agent I want to buy a home?

A. Tell him. Some agents aren't comfortable helping buyers make decisions. Buyers can think the agent doesn't care about them. Not so. These agents just feel helping buyers decide on a home is too pushy. A word of caution: Be sure this type of agent is tough enough to negotiate in your favor. If he's not straightforward enough to ask you to buy, he may not be assertive enough to go to bat for you in the negotiation.

Q. I started chatting with the seller of the home I want to buy. The seller told me the price he'd take, and the terms he would accept. These are much lower and more attractive to me than the price and terms listed in the MLS. What should I do?

A. Get together with your agent and write an offer with the terms the seller told you he'd accept. Don't negotiate verbally with the seller. There could be misunderstandings. Get everything in writing. Remember, too, until you have the seller's signature on the offer, agreeing in writing to all the terms he stated verbally, you haven't bought a home!

10

During the Negotiations

Staying on Top of Your Transaction

You and your agent have partnered to decide on your negotiating strategy and the terms of the agreement. Now, you must entrust the negotiating to your agent. Up to now, so much of what you've done has been the two of you. Suddenly, it's all changed. The agent must act alone. There's no greater responsibility on the agent than that time when he takes the offer to the seller (or presents the offer to the listing agent, whichever is customary in your area). In this chapter, we'll discuss what you should expect from your agent during the negotiating of the transaction, and what you should do if the process starts going sideways. I see that buyers know too little about this part of the process, and sometimes don't know when the agent is doing them a favor—or a disservice. Armed with the information in this chapter, you'll be able to feel in control of the process from offer to agreement.

> ## Insider Secret
> ☞ Your offer may not find its way to the seller nearly as quickly as you thought.

Time Is of The Essence

In a real estate transaction, timing is really important. As soon as your agent and you have completed the offer, your agent should present it. I've seen some agents treat an offer like the old invitation, "let's do lunch." Not very serious, and certainly not impending! Remember, until your offer is presented and signed by the seller, you don't have an agreement. Be sure your agent immediately calls whoever he needs to call in his area to "log in the offer," and arrange to present it. He may need to call the listing agent, the listing office, or the seller. Find out the standard practice in your area. Don't allow your agent to put off presenting the offer for any reason. If he can't present the offer quickly, tell him to find another agent in his office to present the offer, or enlist the manager of the office to present the offer.

Insider Secret

☞ Who's on first? If the listing agent has an offer on the property, it very well may get placed before yours.

The Listing Agent's Role in the Offer Presentation

You've signed the offer. Your agent has notified the listing agency of the offer. In some cases, sellers direct the listing agents to present offers. In some areas, listing agents always present offers. In others, a letter from the seller directing the listing agent to present the offer is required. Check with your agent about the practices of your area. When the listing agent presents the offer, you must be sure that your offer is presented right away, especially if the listing agent also has an offer herself on the property.

Here's what could happen: Your agent drops off the offer at the listing agent's office, and points out that the offer is to be presented that day. The listing agent explains, though, that the sellers are traveling in their motor home. She will have to wait until the sellers call her before she can present the offer. Well, there doesn't seem to be much your agent can do but wait. A week goes by, with no word from the listing agent. Your agent has called the listing agent three times, with no answer. You are getting frantic. Finally, the listing agent calls your agent and informs your agent that the house is sold—but not to his buyers. Well, your agent asks, "How did this happen?" The listing agent explains that she presented *her* offer to the sellers, which they accepted. Smells fishy, doesn't it? And it is. The listing agent did something illegal by not presenting all offers. Why? She wanted to sell the home herself. This kind of maneuvering is not uncommon.

If Your Agent Is Having Communication Problems with the Listing Agent

Following the guidelines in this book, you've chosen a great agent, an agent working at real estate as a full-time career. But, remember, 44 percent of the companies affiliate with part-timers. If the listing agent on the home you want to buy is a part-timer, timely communication becomes difficult. In addition, the listing agent may be playing that sleazy game I just described. What can you do to make sure the seller sees your offer in a timely manner?

- Direct your agent to press hard for an immediate presentation.
- Tell your agent to have her manager call the listing agent's manager.
- Call your agent's manager and demand that he call the listing agent's manager and demand immediate presentation.
- If none of these three solutions help to get your offer presented, call the listing agent's manager and threaten to tell your state department of licensing that it seems the listing agency is violating its fiduciary responsibilities. That should get a response.

One Offer or Many: How Offers Are Presented

Let's say you wrote your offer that morning, and gave the seller until noon to respond. (That, by the way, is a very short time to respond, but it urges the seller to consider your offer fast.) When the agent presented the offer, it was the only offer the seller had in front of him. In that case, the seller might look at your offer and respond by noon. But, let's say another agent calls the seller (or listing agent, whichever is appropriate for your area) at 11:00 AM and says he'd like to present an offer at 1 PM The seller has not signed your offer yet. The seller likely will want to look at both offers to see which one he'd like to respond to. So, he just holds your offer until 1 PM and looks at both offers.

What should you do if your offer is held? You have two choices: You can withdraw your offer at noon by instructing your agent to notify the seller or listing agent that you are doing that. Of course, if you withdraw your offer before the seller has answered you, you can't offer to purchase the home. Or, you can continue to hold out your offer to the seller. Be sure to talk over this time frame issue with your agent, and find out how much urgency you should write into your offer. Also discuss what you would do if there's another offer and the seller wants to look at both offers together.

Getting Your Offer Accepted

Buyers love to think they're the only ones interested in that home at the time. They rarely consider that they may be competing with another buyer. In fact, agents say this is one of the most misunderstand parts of the buying process. If you and your agent have agreed that yours is a competitive market, you'll want to make your offer attractive enough that the seller will want to consider your offer rather than any others he sees at that time. Here's why: Sellers don't usually respond to more than one offer at a time. That is, they won't "counteroffer," or put in writing what they will accept, to two or more buyers at the same time. Why? Because the process gets complicated, and there's always a risk that the seller could end up selling the home to two buyers—or at least get sued because two buyers thought they both bought the home.

This is what happens when a seller has two offers sitting on his desk. One is for full price, with a large deposit, few contingencies, and a fast closing. The other is for $10,000 less than full price, and less attractive terms. Which one do you believe the seller *should* respond to? Of course, the seller will almost always respond to the best offer. When I say "respond," I don't mean necessarily that the seller will sign the offer just as it was presented to the seller. He may create a counteroffer. But, generally, sellers will not respond at all to a lesser offer to see how much those other buyers would be willing to pay for his home! Why should he? Don't be disappointed with your agent if you instruct him to write a noncompetitive offer, and the seller responds to a better offer.

Are You the "Nicer Buyer"?

Sometimes a buyer thinks he can convince a seller to take his low offer because he's "nice." This buyer directs his agent to tell the seller just that. Then, if the seller doesn't buy that line, the buyer tells the agent to confide to the seller that the buyer will pay more. (Remember, to be legal, an offer must be in writing. Saying that to an agent doesn't mean a thing! The agent has no "clout" in passing along your comment to the seller.)

The reason I say this is that I've seen well-meaning agents try to please buyers by assuring them they'll try to get the seller to consider their offer, even though the agent knows that offer probably isn't good enough to get a signature from a seller. Then, when the agent returns to the buyer without a signed offer, the buyer is either mad at the agent or furious at the listing agent, thinking that he was cheated out of a home, by some maneuvering.

If you and your agent believe you will be competing for the home you want, find out how to make your offer attractive enough to be in the running. Sometimes agents recommend your writing two offers. The first is presented, and, if it's not competitive enough, the agent presents your second offer, so that you're more competitive with the other offers. Or, you structure your offer to say you're willing to pay a certain amount over the best offer on the table. Be sure you understand the ramifications of your offer, and that you feel comfortable with the strategies you and your agent decide on.

If Another Offer Is Being Negotiated

A home isn't considered sold (or, in some areas, it's termed a "pending sale," because the sale hasn't closed), until both seller and buyer have agreed, in writing, to the terms of the offer. As long as a buyer and seller are counteroffering, the home isn't sold, and another buyer can get into the fray with his offer. If you want to make an offer on a home that is being negotiated, go ahead. Sometimes lazy listing agents discourage additional offers by telling buyers' agents that the home "has an offer on it," intimating the home is sold, when, in fact, buyer and seller are still negotiating. If your agent calls the listing agent and hears, "There's an offer already on the property," your agent should ask, "Is the offer signed completely by both parties?" If the answer is "no," your agent should arrange to present your offer immediately.

If the home is listed by a sleazebag agent, he may try to fib about the offer having been completely signed—especially if it's his offer! Your offer should be presented while the other buyer and seller are countering (still negotiating), so the seller gets the benefit of seeing all offers, and you get the benefit of attempting to purchase the home.

Counteroffers: Any Response Is Better than None

Sellers' egos are fed by their listing agents—that's how many agents snag a listing. Listing agents have led the sellers to believe that their overpriced homes are worth every penny. If you write a low offer, you have just burst the seller's bubble. In the seller's eyes, you've just insulted him, his wife, his mother, his kids, and anybody and anything else that's dear to him! You've hit him right in the emotions, and it hurts. So, his first reaction is to tell your agent what he can do with that offer (you can imagine). The buyer's agent is so happy to escape the wrath of the seller that he meekly takes the offer back without any indication from the seller, in writing, of what he will accept. This is that flat-out offer rejection I mentioned earlier. What usually happens is the seller screams something at the agent, like, "You tell your buyer to bring me something that won't insult me, or I won't deal with him!"

The problem is that all your agent can relay to you is what the seller said. Most of it was fueled by emotion, and, your agent, feeling hurt, and probably angry at the seller, may convey his feelings to you. How do you feel? The whole thing makes you mad. You are likely to tell your agent what you think the seller can do with that statement (you can imagine that, too). Now, we're not getting anywhere, right?

What should your agent have done? Worked hard to get some indicator, on the offer, of what the seller would accept, so you can deal with it (a counteroffer). In my experience, this counteroffer will be a worse one than the buyer would have gotten if he had not, in the seller's view, "insulted" him. Now, we're negotiating from a bad position. Not only do the parties think the offer and counteroffers are bad, they don't like each other.

What should you do if you find yourself in this situation? Realize how the seller feels. Accept that his counteroffer is high because he's hurt, and don't react to the seller's counteroffer like he reacted to yours. Create a counteroffer to the counteroffer that lets the seller "save face" and gets you back into a reasonable negotiation.

What You Should Expect from Your Agent

There's no greater time of anxiety for a buyer than this period when the offer is being presented. Buyers feel out of control. And, in reality, they are. Generally, the presenting and negotiating is going to be done by your agent. During this time, you, as a buyer, will have little choice but to take your agent's word about what happened in that room when he, the seller's agent, and the seller spoke. How do you know, then, that your agent is working hard to get a signed offer from the seller? Here are the four actions your agent should be taking during this negotiating phase, to ensure that you get the home you want:

1. Present the Offer in a Timely Manner

Your agent should present your offer immediately, so you are in the best negotiating position. If your agent tells you that the offer can't be presented for days, find out why. If it's because your agent just doesn't have time, call your agent's broker. Get that offer presented. If it's because the listing agent won't allow your offer to be presented, find out why. When in doubt, call your agent's broker, or even the listing agent's broker. Remember, stalls from the listing agent usually mean that the listing agency is trying to drum up their own offers to beat you out of the running. Don't stand for it. If your agent gets lily-livered here, call his broker for assistance. You need to get that offer presented.

If you feel your agent is really being thwarted by the listing company, call your state department of licensing. That will make a believer out of the listing agency!

2. Get All Counteroffers in Writing

How quickly should your agent get a counteroffer from the seller? From your point of view, right away. But, what if the seller stalls? You have two choices. You can withdraw your offer, or you can accept the "stall." You should decide with your agent, before your offer is presented, what you want to do in this situation. A good agent will help the seller get a sense of urgency. He may tell the seller that you are still looking at properties. He'll remind the seller that you can withdraw your offer at any time—until a seller has signed it in agreement.

Remember, just because you give a seller until midnight to sign doesn't mean you must keep your offer in front of the seller until that time. Because you made the offer, you can also withdraw it at any time. Be sure you and your agent understand this and agree on what is to happen should the seller stall. If the stall goes on very long, you might want to call the listing agent's broker and find out why you can't get an answer. If the listing agent's broker sounds fishy, tell him you'll check out procedure with your state department of licensing.

3. Communicate with You Promptly

You've made your offer. Now, you're sitting in a hotel room, wondering what's going on. Your agent hasn't called. You don't know if the offer has been presented, countered, and whether you've bought a home. To avoid this situation, agree with your agent before the offer is presented how you'll communicate, and when. Be sure you're available to sign a counteroffer so your offer is still active. Be available, too, to sign a buyer's receipt, to show you accepted the seller's terms.

4. Plan the Entire Offering Strategy

Unfortunately, many agents don't strategize with buyers *before* they write an offer. Strategy, as you've found in these chapters, should include assessing the state of the market, determining market trends, understanding how presentation and counteroffering works in the area, and assessing the vulnerable areas of the seller. Without this

Real Life

I thought I had sold a home to a nice couple, because I got a builder's signature, with one minor change. (The buyers wanted the builder to put a $200 pull-down ladder to the garage attic, at the builder's expense. The builder declined to pay for the ladder.) However, I couldn't find the buyers to get them to initial the change and sign the acceptance to the offer. In the meantime, another agent presented what the builder felt was a better offer (at least $200 better!), and I was informed that the builder was withdrawing his counteroffer to my buyers, and that he had sold the home to someone else. I was devastated! It taught me two lessons: Always know where the buyers are right after the offer is presented, and be willing, as an agent, to buy a pull-down ladder if you can't find the buyers and you think the home is right for them. The end of this story is that the buyers decided they wanted the builder to build a home for them, and they did get a lovely home, but with a lot more work on their part. At least, everyone finally got what they were happy with.

information, buyers just aren't in good negotiating positions. If that's the case, why don't agents strategize with buyers? Many of them don't realize that this is part of their job. Some of them are afraid to tell the buyer something he may not want to hear. They would rather have the goodwill of the buyer, short term, than serve the buyer's best interests long term.

If Your Agent Isn't Responsive to You During Negotiations

If your agent just isn't acting in your best interests during this negotiating process (or at any time during the transaction), you should sit down and be direct with your agent. If you get no results, call his manager. Be aware, though, when you call the manager and complain about the agent, you put the manager in a difficult position. On the one hand, he wants to please you. And, most importantly, he wants to avoid a law-suit. However, if there's a way he can calm you down without address-ing an agent's wrong behavior, he will mostly likely take that route.

To avoid being pacified, here's what I suggest. Before you make the call, jot down your complaint. When you call, be succinct. State the complaint, but don't ask for resolution at that time from the manager. Instead, tell the manager that you want to meet with him and the agent, all in the same room at the same time. Why? Because you don't want the manager to hear your side of the story, then go to the agent, and hear his side, then call you back and tell you nothing's wrong. You want action, or at least open communication and cooperation. Meeting together is also better for the manager, because then he can hear the story from your mouth, and the three of you can decide together the best course of action.

Negotiating for Yourself

Are buyers ever present at the initial offer presentation? Not often. Usually, if you have a good agent negotiator, the agent can be more effective than you. As buyers, we have the tendency to want to be agreeable to the seller. We don't hold our cards close enough to the deck. Or, we let our emotions get in the way of the negotiation, reacting to something a seller says, and creating adversary positions.

However, there are some instances when you may decide it's in your best interest to be at the initial negotiation. It could be you and the seller have become friends, and you feel the goodwill you've created will help both of you. It could be you and the seller insist in sitting down together, because you both feel you must be there. You may not think that either agent is doing you justice. Before you decide you must be in on this initial presentation, discuss strategy with your agent.

Stepping in When Negotiations Bog Down

What about stepping into the negotiation later on? Let's say you feel the negotiation has broken down. You feel, if you could only sit down with the seller, you could work things out. Generally, agents will advise against buyers and sellers sitting down together, for the reasons I listed above. However, sometimes buyers and sellers, when facing each other, become much more understanding and empathetic to each other than they are when they're just talking about each other. It's easy to mouth off about a seller to your agent when you don't have to face the seller. It's easy to feel a sense of bravado, and relay that to your agent. However, sometimes things get more realistic when buyer and seller face each other. Every situation is different. Discuss the pros and cons of facing the seller with your agent. It could be the way past a roadblock. It is tricky, though. The more people involved in the negotiation, the more complicated the negotiation becomes.

It's Almost Your Home Now

Armed with the advice in this chapter, you'll be better able to understand—and control—the negotiation process. You'll know when things are going right, when they're going wrong, and what to do about it. The more you know, the more you communicate and plan with your agent, the better your chances are of getting the home you want—at an attractive price and terms.

Frequently Asked Questions

Q. My agent wrote an offer for me and told me he'd present it that day. However, it's been three days and I haven't heard a word. What should I do?

A. Call your agent now. If he doesn't respond, call his broker. Sometimes, agents have the best of intentions, but they just don't get around to presenting the offer. That could cost you the home of your dreams! The broker will either step in and present your offer, or he'll light a fire under your agent.

Q. I made an offer on a home. The seller was 100 miles from me, and it was 8:00 PM by the time we got the offer finished. So, my agent presented the offer over the phone. The seller agreed with my terms, and said he'd meet my agent the next day to sign the offer. My agent called and told me I'd bought a home. However, the next day, she called and said someone else bought the home. How could that be?

A. Remember, until it's in writing, there is no agreement. It's unfortunate the seller broke his word to you, but, that's his right. He must have received a better offer and decided to sign that offer.

11

Signed, Sealed, and Almost Delivered

Your agent has just called you and told you that the seller accepted your offer. She'll be right over and get your signature on the "purchaser receipt" line. When that happens, you've bought a home! You are so excited. After signing that last piece of paper and getting your receipt, the agent leaves. What happens next? There must be some more really urgent things to do. After all, this negotiating process was so stressful, so time consuming, so exciting. Well, relax. The next part isn't going to be like the negotiating part.

In contrast, it's going to be boring, and, I hope, predictable. It should be, because the "processing" of the transaction, all that paperwork that occurs from now until closing, needs to be handled in an orderly fashion, to ensure you actually get ownership to that home.

Recognizing Buyer's Remorse

There's an initial exhilaration of knowing you just bought a home. Then, another feeling can set in. Agents call this feeling "buyer's remorse." After the agent leaves, you and Martha sit down and reality starts to set in. You actually *bought* a home. You just didn't try to buy a home. You bought it. Now you start the worries. How will you make the payments? After all, they'll be $200 more than you're paying for rent. How will you furnish the home? You'll need at least $10,000 in furniture (and, the more you think about it, the more expensive it gets). You and Martha list all the moving costs, the landscaping costs, the new drapes needed. The more you think about the cost, the more over-whelming the purchase seems.

After you exhaust yourself with costs, you turn to the choice of home. You remember all those other homes you saw. Shouldn't you have looked at more homes? After all, there may be something out there better than the home you picked as your "dream home." You're talking yourself out of your purchase. Now, admittedly, you and your agent went over all the points above, but, before the purchase your deci-sion seemed so rational. However, you don't feel rational; you feel fear-ful. Finally, at 3:00 AM, after having been wide awake all night, you call your agent, waking her from a dreamless, and exhausted sleep. You blurt out, "We want to get out of our offer! We made a mistake. How can we get our deposit back?"

I hope your agent is experienced, so she knows this is a classic case of buyers' remorse, and doesn't overreact. It's absolutely human and predictable that any of us, in the reality of knowing that we spent all that money, and will have those house payments for the next 30 years, would feel some panic. Your agent's job is to review (the next day, not at 3:00 AM), with you all your considerations, putting them back into the context you created prior to making your offer. Then, you'll feel much more in control of the situation, and realize that you don't have to spend all those thousands of dollars the minute you move into your new home. Just taking it one step at a time ensures that buyer's remorse, along with that panicky feeling, will subside. If you have gone through the process I've described in this book, you've made a good decision.

You Relax; Others Go to Work

Being sure all the papers are in order and that buyer and seller are paying and receiving the right amounts of money is the responsibility of various professionals now. This process takes from four to six weeks, on average. When their work is finished, you can give your money to the seller and receive the papers showing the home has been transferred to you, the proud new owner. Here's a quick run-through of what happens during this time:

- Seller proves he has a clear title to the property.
- Financial institution approves the loan.

- Monetary prorations and adjustments for seller and buyer.
- Buyer pays the seller money due to him.
- Seller signs the deed.
- Buyer gets keys to the property.
- The deed is recorded in the buyer's name.

How to Be a "Model" Borrower

The successful closing of a property, the process by which you become the legal owner, depends greatly on your cooperation for completion. You'll be asked to provide information in a timely manner to the mortgage and escrow companies. Because almost all mortgage loans are sold to a business that collects the payments, your loan must qualify as "salable." That means you must meet all of the criteria this buyer of loans wants. So, when you apply for a loan, you may feel you're giving away your deepest, darkest secrets. You'll probably feel as though you don't have any secrets left. You'll probably feel that the whole process is unfair. Don't those moneybags loaning you money know you're honest? Don't they know you're good for your word? Face it. They don't care. They just want evidence, on paper, that you're a low risk. So you don't want to reveal all of your financial status. Tough. If you want the home, you must reveal. Frequently, the buyer gets to this point and refuses to get the information to the loan officers and loan processor needed to get that loan approved. You just don't have any bargaining power here. If you want the home, and the loan officer needs the information, get the information to the loan officer ASAP.

I've seen buyers, too, drag their feet in filling out forms, signing releases, finding necessary papers, because they just don't have a sense of urgency at this point. Well, buyers, keep that sense of urgency. The purchase and sale agreement has dates for completion in it. Sellers have made plans based on the buyer's promise to get financing and close by a certain date. When buyers act lackadaisical about the loan process, they put their home purchase in jeopardy. More than that, in my opinion, they're violating the promises they made to sellers. How would you like it, if, as a seller, you made your plans to take your sales proceeds and move to Australia on March 1, but your buyer just hadn't gotten around to completing his paperwork for the loan process? You would feel as though the buyer had violated your trust.

The Role of Your Agent as Your Loan Is Processed

Chances are, while you were zeroing in on the home of your choice, you were talking to your agent frequently, even several times a day. Now, that's not the case. Instead, you're talking with the other parties involved such as the inspector, the loan officer, and the loan processor. Your agent should also be talking with these people, to ensure that each is doing his job in a timely manner. At least weekly, your agent should touch base with you. Your agent also should keep the listing agent informed of your progress. If problems arise, your agent should take whatever actions needed to get the problem into the hands of the person who can provide the solution. If you don't hear from your agent at least weekly, touch base with him. Your agent should be giving you regular reports on the progress of your transaction.

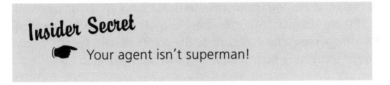

Insider Secret

☞ Your agent isn't superman!

What Your Agent Can Do to Solve Problems in the Transaction

If problems arise during this processing period, don't expect your agent to have superhuman powers to make the parties do what you want done. Here's an example: The seller has agreed to fix the fence, which is leaning dangerously at the back of the property. This is to be at the seller's expense, and the repair is supposed to be finished by a certain date. You happen to drive by the home in the evening two days before the deadline date (well, you happen to drive by every evening, to tell the truth). You see, to your frustration, that the seller hasn't fixed the fence. You call your agent and demand that he make the seller get that fence repaired. Yes, you think your agent walks on water, or wears a cape, because he has done such a fine job for you. But, here's where any power ends. Since your agent isn't a party to the agreement, he can't enforce the agreement. He can't say anything to force a seller to take actions the seller won't take.

What should happen now? First, since the seller has one more day to get that fence repaired, nothing bad has happened—yet. Your agent might call the listing agent just to remind him that there is one more day to fix that fence. The listing agent, though, has no enforcement power, either, with the seller. I bring up this point because buyers—and sellers—look to their agents to make the parties to the transaction *do something*. If the agent, to keep the goodwill of the buyer, says, "I'll try," the buyer, of course, thinks the agent just promised to *make* the seller get it done. When the agent, of course, can't make the seller take action, and reports this back to the buyer, the buyer is furious—at the agent. Many agents fall into this trap, especially new ones.

Get a clear understanding with your agent, during this time, about what the agent can and can't do to facilitate the closing of the transaction. What the agent can, and should do during the processing of the transaction, is to be sure everyone knows what is to be accomplished by a certain date, and communicate those accomplishments to all parties. If there are problems, the agent's job is to communicate the problem to the person who can provide the solution. The agent's job cannot be to fix something he is unable or powerless to fix.

If You Want Possession Prior to Your Possession Date in the Agreement

When is the home yours to occupy? Many buyers believe they have occupancy rights to the property the minute they find out they have an agreement with the seller. Wrong. Until proceeds from the sale are available to the seller and the sale is recorded the buyer doesn't own the property. Buyers have no right to be on the property prior to the possession date listed in their agreement. Usually that's closing, but, sometimes, purchase and sale agreements state that buyers will have possession a certain number of days (anywhere from 3 to 30 and beyond) after closing. (Be sure to check your agreement for possession dates).

To occupy before the time stated in the purchase and sale agreement, buyers must execute a written "occupancy prior to closing" (rental) agreement with the seller. Agents, though, to please buyers, sometimes give buyers a key to the property so they can, as they explain, "measure for drapes." Then, the agent discovers the buyer has moved his belongings in, sometimes along with himself! Not only is this a violation of trust with the seller, it's risky legally for a buyer. So, buyers, just don't even think about asking for a key until you have removed all your contingencies, and have either signed a rental agreement with the seller, or have legal possession of the property as stated in your purchase and sale agreement.

Insider Secret
☛ There may be 50 ways to leave your lover, but there's *one* way to really bug a seller.

Respect the Seller's Right to His Property

I know you're excited about moving into your new home. You want to move tomorrow. The next best thing is to visit the home every so often. That's a good way, though, to alienate the seller. Now, you may think that seller would be really understanding. After all, you want your move-in to be trouble-free. You want to make a cute little diagram of how you'll place your furniture. You want to try out paint swatches in the baby's room to be sure that color you're thinking of is just right. Make it easy for you, right?

But, the seller has other things on his mind. He has to move, too. He's got all the challenges you've got. Generally, he's understanding enough of your needs to let you come over once. But, that's about it. Don't push it. After all, you need cooperation from that seller. You want him to leave the property in a reasonable condition. You don't want to have to mow one month's worth of grass in the summer. If you overextend your welcome, you may take any feelings of goodwill away the seller has had for you.

It's Almost Your Home

It's three days until closing, when you get possession. Your loan has been approved, and you're arranging to get moving. The seller has moved out, and you want to reinspect the home. So, you call your agent and together, you drive to the home. To your dismay, you find the grass has been uncut for the past month. Then, as you enter the home, you see that the seller has left two dumpsters worth of garbage. This is *not* what you expected! This is not the condition in which you bought the home. What should you do? Can you get your agent to force the seller to do what you have expected him to do?

Remember what I said about your agent's power, and what your agent couldn't do? Here is a time when we agents wish we had unlimited power. So many times, we get right to closing and the seller (or buyer) reneges on promises made—either promises explicitly in writing, or promises made in goodwill. Regardless of whether the promise was in writing, we have a problem when the parties to the transaction don't do what they said they would. Your agent, at this point, can call the listing agent, and ask that the listing agent call the seller and remind him that he signed an agreement to leave the property in the same condition it was when you signed the offer.

By this time, the seller probably has little interest in coming back, doing yard work, and hauling away two dumpster loads. What can be done? You can refuse to close, so the seller can't get the proceeds. But, you can't move in then, either. When you come to this kind of impasse, talk over your options with your agent. When all else fails, I suggest you contact a real estate attorney. You're ready now for some threatened legal recourse. I'm not suggesting you sue that seller, only that you talk to an attorney to assess your options. Generally, an attorney will suggest that she write a letter on your behalf, stating what you expect to happen, and what will happen if the seller doesn't do what he promised to do in the agreement. Then, if you don't get the response you want from the seller, you can decide your next step.

Deciding on your priorities.   When you're angry because a seller broke a promise, this next argument might offend you. However, it's the perspective in which you must put your problem. Is it worth delaying moving into your home, to make a seller mow the lawn? Who really wins? I just used the lawn example because it really happened in our office. There are countless examples of situations where sellers let buyers down. But, when buyers have gone after sellers for relatively minor costs, buyers raise their stress levels even more—and deplete their pocketbooks.

Yes, it's wrong for sellers to leave properties in poorer condition than the buyer expected. It's wrong for sellers to take plants they promised to leave. It's wrong for sellers to fib about a stove element that they said worked—but didn't. Buyers have legal recourse to these wrongs. Just be sure it's worth it, and that you won't pay more in attorneys' fees than you recover from the seller. The key to avoiding unwanted surprises is for you and your agent to get in writing your expectations of the seller in the offer. Even then, the nicest, most cooperative sellers become irresponsible when their stress levels go up, and their bank account dwindles as they struggle under the weight of their moving costs.

What to Expect of Your Agent after You Move In

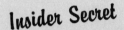

Insider Secret

☞ After closing, some agents disappear.

You now own your home. You've moved in. Are you ever going to see your agent again? That depends. If you have chosen the kind of agent I've suggested in this book, chances are you'll see your agent for many years after your sale has closed. Your agent will call or visit you shortly after you move into your home. He'll probably bring a little something as a house-warming present, just to let you know that he cares about you. Your agent will continue calling you after this, just to be sure that everything is okay. You'll receive postcards or perhaps a newsletter from this agent. You see, to this agent, you're an important business relationship. And, better than that, this agent enjoys and respects the friendship that was nurtured during the buying process.

The Benefits of Keeping in Touch with Your Agent

Buyers feel the real proof that their agent cares more about them than just the commission is when the agent stays in touch—forever. If something goes wrong with your property after move-in, you'll want to talk with your agent. If you have a good relationship with your agent, and your agent has kept in touch, you'll feel comfortable talking over your situation. If, however, your agent hasn't kept in touch, you'll feel awkward calling him with your problems.

What You Can Do for Your Agent

In my opinion, finding a competent agent is worth thousands of dollars to you. It's wonderful when grateful buyers reciprocate an agent's efforts by helping them build their businesses. When you find a competent agent, make sure that others have an opportunity to work with him. Be generous with referring buyers (and sellers) to your agent. That's what a good agent works for. It's not the money, it's not the sale. It's the satisfied customers referring others to the agent, that helps the agent build a strong business (and makes the business emotionally rewarding and fun).

Home Sweet Home

The real estate business is in a state of great change, as you read in this book. You can sort through the confusion by following the buying process I've outlined here. Gathering information early, interviewing and qualifying potential agents, and choosing a competent agent all ensure you'll start the process right. The end result is that using the insider secrets in this book, you'll stay in control of your buying process and find the perfect property for you. Here's to you as you find the home of your dreams. I'm glad I could help.

Frequently Asked Questions

Q. I had a water leak after I moved into my home. When I looked at the area around the leak, I could see that there had been earlier water damage from before I moved in. However, the sellers said nothing about water damage during the negotiations. I want the sellers to pay for the repair. How do I tell them?

A. Since you're the owner of the property now, you have the most clout in convincing the sellers to pay for that repair. Call your agent and get the phone number of the sellers. When you talk to the seller, be polite but firm. Why am I not recommending that your agent call the seller? Because you have more power, since you're the owner.

Q. I signed the final papers on this property and moved into my home three weeks ago, but my agent hasn't contacted me since we talked a few days prior to passing papers (closing). Is this normal?

A. Unfortunately, yes. Many agents feel the relationship is over once the buyer becomes the owner. As you can tell from this book, I don't agree with that attitude. I think agents should keep buyers for life, staying in contact frequently. Not only is that a good business decision, it's also a good "people" decision. I know you won't be sending any referrals your agent's way!

Other Helpful Sources of Information

Video

Agency Relationships in Buying or Selling a Home. Creative Learning Concepts, 1220 S. Jefferson, Sioux Falls, SD 57105. To order, call 605-338-8022. $30.

CDs

Know the Neighborhood. Locates any geographic area of the country. Includes street maps, landmarks, crime rates, public housing records, schools, climate reports, snapshots of neighborhoods, and neighborhood comparisons with local, national averages. Lysias, Inc., 2300 Computer Ave., Suite C-13, Willow Grove, PA, 19090. To order, call 1-800-975-9742.

On the Web

Information about Purchasing a Home

International Real Estate Directory, at http://www.ired.com. This comprehensive site includes real estate information, financing, real estate agents available, searchable directory, properties available internationally, and news from Inman News Service.

A New Home, at http://www.anewhome.com. Includes everything related to buying or selling a new home.

American Homeowners Association, HOMECentral, at http:// www.ahahome.com. Includes home-related information, products, services, as well as information on how to buy, finance, and maintain your home.

Homebuyer's Fair, at http://www.homefair.com. Includes interactive software for mortgages and relocation.

Real Estate OnNet, at http://www.realestateonnet.com. Includes information about purchasing and selling.

National Association of REALTORS®, at http:/www.realtor.com. Includes information on homebuying and choosing an agent, and features a database of over 1 million homes.

Government Services Administration, at http://www.gsa.gov. Features homebuying tips from the U.S. Government.

The U.S. Department of Housing and Urban Development (HUD), at http://www.hud.gov. Includes information for low-income buyers, and home listings from HUD and VA, FHA loan programs.

Information about Mortgages

Countrywide Home Loans, Inc., at http://www.countrywide.com. Features a glossary and interactive prequalification forms.

Fannie Mae, at http://www.fanniemae.com. The Federal National Mortgage Association provides new mortgage information and related reports.

InfoBank—Bank Rate Monitor, at http://www.bank-rate.com. This publisher tracks bank rates and features personal finance information and a loan calculator.

Mortgage Mart, at http://www.mortgagemart.com. This page features information on the mortgage application process, articles and calculators, and allows users to search for mortgage companies by city.

Information about Schools

SchoolMatch, at http://ppshost.schoolmatch.com/oldindx.htm. This page provides statistics and news about education; reports are available for a fee.

Information about Home Inspections

American Society of Home Inspectors, at http://www.ashi.com. This page provides home inspection tips, ASHI home inspectors in your area, and information on what to expect from an inspector.

Information about Properties

CyberHomes, at http://www.cyberhomes.com/. This page provides street-level mapping and links for communities nationally.

Homes and Land Magazine, at http://www.homes.com. This home page for a national magazine features property listings.

HomeNet Real Estate Service, at http://www.netprop.com/homenet.htm. This page provides links to property listings and school and community information.

HomeScout, at http://homescout.com/. Provides access to over 500,000 real estate listings from over 250 listings sites worldwide.

The Living Network, at http://usa.living.net/. Operated by the Florida Association of REALTORS®, this page provides links to each state Association and information on properties and buying.

Index